WAYNE PUBLIC LIBRARY, NJ

T5-CRY-659

391.07
KUNCIOV, ROBERT
MR. GODEY'S LADIES

WAYNE PUBLIC LIBRARY

MAIN LIBRARY

475 Valley Road

Wayne, N. J. 07470

Books may be returned at any
branch of the library.

JAN 9 1980

MR. GODEY'S LADIES

Mr. Godey's Ladies

Being a Mosaic of Fashions & Fancies

Edited by Robert Kunciov

BONANZA BOOKS · NEW YORK

Copyright © MCMLXXI by The Pyne Press

Library of Congress Catalog Card Number 79-162364

All rights reserved.

This edition is published by Bonanza Books
a division of Crown Publishers, Inc.
by arrangement with The Pyne Press

b   c   d   e   f   g   h

Manufactured in the United States of America

CHRONOLOGY

Fashions creep into vogue and out again with such stealth that the center of popularity can only be approximated. This chronology, consequently, is variable and by no means all-inclusive.

1830's

1830 Light colors such as blues, lilacs and yellows popular. Taffetas, organdies, satins and silks used most frequently. Wasp waists were emphasized by large belts; skirts were full. Other appurtences: leg of mutton sleeves with feather cushions or wicker frames to puff them out; shoulder line sloping; berthas and square shawls; cabriolet bonnets.

1833 Velvet popular for everything. Shoes were flat with square toes. Hair was worn with curls, frequently supported by a wire frame or tortoise-shell combs. Heart-shaped bodices were in vogue.

1834 Fabrics were more precious: satin, velvets, lace especially favored. Sleeves were full to the waist, often puffed twice. Bonnets were still large and flowing.

1835 Prints and brocades became a vogue. Elaborate detail began to appear on small articles such as handkerchiefs. Collars were worn low and turned over. Cashmere shawls were highly desirable. Horsehair tissue was still worn under petticoats for padding.

1836   The fad of the year — bonnets with violet and green rib-bon. Fussy blonde lace was extremely fashionable. Grecian coif-fures were popular. Short gloves were worn with embroidered tops.

1838   Straw hats enter into vogue for the next few years. Hair is worn with ringlets rather than in Grecian style. The first manu-factured watches are terribly stylish.

1840's

1840   The equestrian look is "in" with riding habits. Neck and shoulders are bare, especially on evening dresses, the tops of which may be decorated with a profusion of flowers and ribbons. Crino-lines come into fashion with as many as five or six petticoats with body padding considered normal. Long shawls, spencers, and scoop bonnets are popular. Gloves are fashionable indoors and mittens may be worn for meals. Very little neck jewelry despite low neckline; occasionally a brooch. Colors are generally light: blues, pinks, fawn, etc.

1841   Serpent bracelets are the "in" thing in jewelry. Evening dresses have very full skirts piled with ruffles and flounces. Hair is piled in elaborate coiffures.

1842   Skirts are growing even larger over very full crinolines, but fabrics are light-weight. The most popular colors are delicate greys and purples.

1843   Dresses are long in back, and mantillas are in vogue.

1844   Floral wreaths dress the hair.

1845   Shoulders become wider, aided by larger berthas and shawls. Skirts increase further in fulness and petticoats are stiffly starched. The flounces deepen and increase in number.

1846   The invention of the sewing machine leads to increased frippery on skirts. Hat styles return to those of the eighteenth century for a short time, and folding parasols are unfurled.

1848   Tints of colors are popular, as well as redingotes.

1850's

1850 Flounces become the outstanding characteristic on skirts throughout the decade in every possible variation: ruffled, wide, narrow, pinked, fringed, flower-bedecked, beribboned. Knitted flowers popular, and browns and shades are favored. Basques are worn with every possible kind of skirt. Lace shawls enjoy a vogue.

1851 Bloomers!! Skirts are three-quarter length over or tucked.

1852 Fabrics grow richer: gauzes, tulles, woolens, organdies, brocades. Darker colors become increasingly popular.

1853 Velvet is *the* fabric.

1854 Hair ornaments made from the lock of a loved and/or departed one and shaped into rings, earrings, bracelets and brooches begin a popularity which would last through the century. Strapless evening gowns are the latest things. Hoop skirts reappear, and deep collars, berthas and cashmere shawls are in vogue.

1855 The height of fashion — pagoda sleeves, a series of false sleeves narrowing at the shoulder. Bonnets and hats increase in size, some with ostrich feathers, and white muslin caps are suggested for indoors.

1858 Inlaid fans of ivory, coral, and mother-of-pearl are most desirable. Hair is now massed loosely in the popular "torsade" and enclosed by a net fringed with pearls. Ruffled dresses have at least a half-dozen flounces at the knee; sleeves are tailored and collars are deep.

1859 Revolutionary ferment grips the fashion world with Garibaldi blouses. The iniquitous hair curlers begin to replace curling papers.

1860's

1860 The triangular feminine fashion shape reaches its apex with a small hat on top of a fitted bodice and huge crinoline. Tiny jockey hats are popular and hairdos tumble like waterfalls. Onyx is popular for jewelry and black velvet chokers with pendants constrict the neck.

1863 Waists have become ridiculously miniscule, and lead to serious breathing problems. The delicate butterfly has become a popular motif. Hairnets of the wearer's own strands are manufactured. Cambric handkerchiefs with colored borders are a fad.

1866 Parasols are raised everywhere and are fringed, beribboned, flowered and/or embroidered. Dress is less full with dress-improvers and bustles coming into style; crinolines have declined considerably. Small trains and form-fitted bodices appear.

1867 The fashionable colors are greens as well as blues and greys.

1868 Trains increase and crinolines are all but dead. Zouave jackets make their faddish appearance. Underskirts are risqués displayed as the over skirt is gathered by fasteners. Richer fabrics are becoming more popular, and tassled boots are being worn.

1870's

1870 Patent leather is introduced. Waist and hips become increasingly closely-fitted until mid-decade. Sleeves fall over the hand and the tunic begins its reign of popularity. Over-dresses are popular, as are small and flat hats loaded with decoration. Curls are massed at the back of the head.

1878 The bustle reaches its final and absurd length. The average waist measurement is 16″ to 17″.

1879 Petticoats begin a new popularity.

"The Lady's Book! How vastly rare!
Are the rich treasures gathered there!"

On a typically humid Philadelphia July day in 1830 *Godey's Lady's Book* began its sixty-eight year reign as America's great fashion magazine. During its years of popularity the publisher, Louis A. Godey, and the magazine's more famous editrix, Mrs. Sarah Josepha Hale, made it a source of the last word in fashion, a compendium of practical advice, an anthology of stories and poems, a gallery of fashion plates and art engravings, a platform of causes *célèbre* and *pas de célèbre* for the unliberated woman, a mirror of grace, and a minor social history. It was found in boudoirs and sitting rooms from the oldest cities of the East to the youngest villages of the frontier.* Coy maids and pious matrons created new bonnets and learned crafts from the latest issue. Their masculine escorts vented their opinions in letters and anecdotes on the pages at the back. Would-be authors, literate and illiterate, published their poems and stories there. In all, for much of the century, it was what its publisher liked to call it: *The* Book.

Its first issue was relatively unpretentious. There was a water-colored fashion plate, one copied after the plates popular in similar French periodicals such as *La Mode, Galerie des Moeurs,* or *Album des Salons.* There were some stories and poems, and there were bits of advice and fashion intelligence—all to be had for a mere three dollars a year.**

---

* *Godey's* reached its highest circulation just before the Civil War with 150,000 readers. By 1873, when it was outdistanced by *Graham's* and *Peterson's* magazines, the number had dropped to 100,000.

** Subscriptions remained at three dollars until after the Civil War when magazines like *Graham's* and *Peterson's* overtook *Godey's* in popularity. The club system was then introduced to hawk the periodical and reduced the subscription to two dollars; a woman who with four of her friends subscribed together had formed a "ten-dollar" club, etc.

The colored fashion plates remained single for the first thirty years. After 1861, however, double plates which had to be folded to fit the octavo volume were produced. Then as many as five figures dressed in the latest styles appeared, artificially posed against a background of a country or garden scene or an interior with its appropriate draperies, furniture, and decor. These were always watercolored at home or in the shop by women hired specifically for the purpose. At one point 150 ladies did the work, using another color for a dress when the first ran out and, by the practice, causing periodic consternation on the part of the readers. The subsequent complaints about the discrepancy between one woman's fashion plate and her neighbor's were met graciously by the publisher who would reply wisely that the choice of colors should be dictated not by fashion but as they suit one's complexion. The plates were accurate in their delineation of the period's fashions, though, and were constantly praised for their beauty. Mr. Godey, the expert at puffery that he was, printed all of the letters he received praising the plates and the magazine, occasionally including tongue-in-cheek comments like that of the Tennessee farmer who, tired of the monotony of women in every plate, pleaded for some variety by the inclusion of bankers, omnibus boys, and starving poets.

In addition to the fashion plates, the magazine used engravings by such great American artists as John Sartain for pictures of all the sentimental subjects we associate with the period — blond children, sighing maidens, famous personages, and pastoral scenes. During the years of subscription battles, these or chromo-lithographs were offered framed as incentives to buy *Godey's*. More often, however, women and men tore out the plates from the issues to enhance their homes and apartments, and today a perfect run of the magazine with illustrations intact appears in only a few libraries. In both the "embellishments," as historian Frank Luther Mott calls them, and the fashion plates the practice of borrowing from foreign journals lasted only a short time. *Godey's* was American enough to use American artists for both.

The number of stories and poems increased in later issues just as the number of plates and embellishments, though on the whole the literary character of the magazine would not compete with *Graham's* or aspire to more than mediocrity. There were the unknowns with their sentimental drip and syrupy contributions— tales and poems which always held virtue in esteem and whose characters elaborated their morals in sickening perorations. Their embellishments were equally fée. But there were also those who would become famous in their day and ours. Ralph Waldo Emerson and Horace Greeley contributed essays; Edgar Allen Poe, criticism; Henry Wadsworth Longfellow and Charles Leland were among the poets; and fiction was offered by Harriet Beecher Stowe, James Kirk Paulding, Herman Melville, and Nathaniel Hawthorne. There was some excellence.

The plates, embellishments, and literature certainly acted to puff the magazine, but they were also part of an oblique supplement to a woman's education, a tutelage of two sorts. The first, more traditional home education, came in the kinds of articles and features Godey's presented to its readers. There were articles on painting, music, poetry, and drama. There were book reviews and biographies of famous women, held up as paragons of virtue or as examples of wickedness. There was history, not only of fashion, but of the world. Travel notes caught the fancy of many who sought a way out of the kitchen. Pictures of draperies and furniture often appeared as did plans and illustrations of model cottages, tantalizing a new bride or frustrating an old maid. An American woman had to be strong, so there were articles on physical fitness, regimens of exercise, series on croquet, horsemanship, and other sports appropriate for the gentler sex. New songs with music and lyrics often appeared on an opening page. Mimes for the home and playlets for children could be found in the back, The philosophy of education made its way into essays. Gardening advice, recipes for the kitchen and boudoir, games, anecdotes, humor, conundrums, chemistry experiments, patterns for toddlers' clothes, and kitchen efficiency could be discovered in the columns. There were crafts: feather painting, painting on glass or velvet, hair work, weaving, crocheting, and knitting. Etiquette and answers to questions on manners were taken up. Only one thing was missing. There was no mention of the questions of the day, of politics or social evils.

During the sixties, one would never have known that the country was at war if one read Godey's; and when the country had gone to insane extremes memorializing its assassinated president, only a small memorial appeared in the back of the recent issue. After all, a woman's domain was the home and not in the ranks of those who fought for social justice or whistle-stopped. Politics and the problems of society were beyond her comprehension.

That philosophy had begun to lose its underpinnings by the late 1860's. With the new attitude of involvement came another type of education for the readers of *Godey's*, an incentive to be actively engaged in matters outside the home. It is through the comments of Sarah Josepha Hale in her "Editor's Table" column that we begin to see the emergence of the liberated woman. Through her efforts the Bunker Hill Monument was erected. She was influential in creating the first public playground and day-nurseries. The readers of *Godey's* heard her urge the admission of women to the medical profession, the uniform celebration of Thanksgiving Day which Lincoln proclaimed in 1863, the acceptance of women missionaries and teachers, and the creation of normal academies. For years she supported Vassar, serving for a term on its board. She was responsible for the physical fitness articles which appeared at regular intervals. In addition, she acted as a model of fashion and grace, and thus not only reflected the growing strength of a woman, but exemplified her dignity. Despite her accomplishments and her efforts to reorient her audience toward a new purpose, she is largely forgotten. She left her impression, as she did her most famous poem, "Mary Had A Little Lamb," to be remembered nevertheless.

But haven't we forgotten something? Wasn't *Godey's* a fashion magazine? Indeed it was, and a gallery of the fads and standard dress of the day. It is really that focus that concerns *Mr. Godey's Ladies* in the larger view of the magazine. Certainly the following pages will show much of the fashion and frivolity of the day, but the tutored eye, like the gentleman whose glance has been caught by a passing woman, will note much that gives the dress its substance beneath. There will be a panorama of dress from the 30's to the late 70's, from the flowing bonnet to the bustle. For the greater part the styles will reflect the fashion abroad. American women took their time in innovating and still do. They would only achieve their goal of shucking off the ties of foreign fashion at the end of the century. Effects of the industrial age and inventions such as the sewing machine will be seen in the overloaded frippery of some periods. The necessity of attracting a man when war had decimated the population of eligible suitors or when the cost of living skyrocketed shows in several decades by raised skirts, slim waists, and an increasing use of cosmetics. Victorianism, once securely rooted, will surface in the disquieted elegance of women late in the period.

The faint odor of attar of roses or lavendar water, a slip of faded ribbon marking a page, colors such as "Frightened Mouse," a valentine poem tucked into a margin, the whisper of silk and a

4

hush of lace, the stray dried petals of a camellia — all vie for our memories when we open an old, tattered copy of *Godey's Lady's Book*. If we ignore those bits of the past, our eyes are caught by a copper or steel engraving of a little dog, white and curly, held closely by a blond cherub with eyes cast heavenward, framed by roses and daisies. On another page a fashion plate full of posing ladies, frail of hand and daintily footed, makes us smile. We may stop for a moment to read a poem or two like "When Sweet Death Ye Shall Steal My Love" or to peruse the tale of a heart which froze with sorrow. Still further there is fashion advice for the month or the latest description of a dress worn by the Queen. There is an outraged letter from some gentleman on the newest fad. Another asks for a recipe mentioned in the day's gossip. An article gives notice of Vassar's progress or the founding of a women's normal academy in New Jersey. The latest recipe for breath sweetener moves us to laughter. We think about trying the "Cold Veal" lately described. And after an hour we put the book aside or return it to its shelf, nostalgic and entertained.

It is history which we ought not to forget. Certainly the serendipitous flowers and ribbon and stray love letters are gone from the following pages, but the substance is not. Matters of space have necessitated the omission of stories and art plates, and many minor omissions were made for a specific focus on the main interest of the original. What is here, however, is not just fashion history — a view of the fancies and foibles of ubiquitous vanity. What follows is a mosaic of *Godey's*, a social history of the American woman in the last century, sociably put.

All quotations are from the text of *Godey's Lady's Book* during the years 1830 to 1879. In many instance spelling discrepancies will be noted. They are a part of the inconsistency of the day. In commentary they have been modernized and a standard form has been used. In some instances I have paraphrased material, shortened, or retold an anecdote from the magazine in deference to space, as in the tale of the carrot coiffure at the end of the book. Any inaccuracies in transcription which appear inadvertently are mine own and no other's. Only one exception to the source of quotations has been made. A number of especially pertinent vignettes have been culled from John Watson's *Annals of Philadelphia, and Pennsylvania*, 3 vols. (Philadelphia, 1857), and have been included for their masculine humor, observation, and general dyspeptic attitudes. All illustrations throughout the text were chosen for their delineation of the fashions and their visual clarity. The fashion plates were selected similarly. In the latter occasional color irregularity may appear; it is to be found in the originals and is in no way a fault of reproduction.

To a great extent, appreciation must go to Edwin Wolf II of The Library Company of Philadelphia for his initial encouragement and for his graciousness in lending the library's set of *Godey's Lady's Book* for the reproduction of the colored plates. Early in my research Lillian Tonkin and Edward Hughes, also of The Library Company, provided valuable time to ferret out secondary materials and to reproduce them. Design of the book is Quentin Fiore's, for which I give much thanks, but his valuable suggestions were also later incorporated into the text, as were those of my best advisor, Lawrence Grow. Finally, special appreciation goes to Eileen Regan who helped with the indexing, gave valuable advice on the various stages of the book, and was, in all, a model of patience.

Robert Kunciov

Germantown, Pennsylvania

"Dress plainly; the thinnest soap-bubbles wear the gaudiest colors."

* * *

THROUGHOUT THE OLD WORLD, the fashions are set by the *courts,* and those who consider themselves the porcelain towers of society . . . But here, in our Republic, on each man and woman rests the responsibility which free citizenship imposes. Here we have the opportunity of consulting individual taste, without reference to any arbitrary standard of high rank to sanction the adoption of extravagant, inconvenient, or immodest modes, and we should be careful that our fashions are not inconsistent with good sense and pure morals."

* * *

"We Americans — *European Americans* I mean — are exactly without *costume,* for no people, taking them as a mass, have so many clothes to put on, but we are a people without a *national costume.*"

* * *

"We have constantly endeavoured to improve the taste of our country women by the influence of the 'Lady's Book' . . . We strive to render the constant influence of the work under our care a source of pure, gentle, and healthful improvement of the whole character of our sex. We do not aim to form or encourage Amazons to go forth as champions against existing evils; but good intelligent, true-hearted women, who will make their own homes the abodes of virtue and happiness."

H! HOW SOFTLY the romantic thirties passed with their bright but soft colors, soft sighs, and softening fashions. Sleeves had changed from the top-heavy leg-of-mutton to ones tighter to the arm; skirts had grown. The women of fashion cast off their pallor as they approached a new era, having previously chased the stray blush by over-powdering or by drinking large amounts of chalk and vinegar. The bonnet, like those on the page opposite, had been the important item, for it proved the best defense against vulgar and stray looks from beaux and simultaneously allowed its wearer a certain coyness. The coy, sighing, romantic lass began to change to a sentimental and demure woman.

As the decade turned into another, so too did the fashions and habits of those who had cast off their pallors. The advent of industry split classes; toil was seen as vulgar. Those who did were the "great unwashed"; those who didn't became the "white collars." Elias Howe would patent a sewing machine; the first telegraph would start its ticking. Byron was found in every boudoir; Dickens reigned in the sitting room. Sentiment, sentimentality, and sense were virtues. Etiquette manuals, with the fashionable woman's help, would turn manners into ritual. Speech once endured by maids in the era past would turn monosyllabic, polished, refined. Patriarchs ruled the family and the husband would be addressed as "Mr." A woman demured.

And demure she was, hiding her complexion from the harsh sun by a parasol, over-clothing herself from the elements, and shrieking "when a grasshopper steps across her path or a cow stops to gaze at her." She wore ringlets, a bonnet, and a quiet dress. The colors were subdued by comparison to the previous decade. Mourning garments were a part of every woman's wardrobe. Mantles, shawls and jackets were worn over a molded bodice, shaped largely by the heavy underclothes beneath. Bell-shaped sleeves grew and grew, exposing a puffed white undersleeve out of which peeked a small hand, white and dainty. The skirts, growing in fullness, exposed a tiny toe, no more. Flounces became a rage and grew in number throughout the age. There was nothing bold.

✿ ✿ ✿

"Diaries.—Every young lady who aspires to the dignity of a well-cultivated mind should keep a diary; say from the time she is fifteen till she reaches the regulated age of twenty-five."

✿ ✿ ✿

"Why is a kiss like a rumor?—Because it goes from mouth to mouth."

"A black bonnet with white feathers, with white, rose, or red flowers, suits a fair complexion. A lustreless white bonnet does not suit well with fair and rosy complexions . . . A light blue bonnet is particularly suited to the light-haired type . . . A green bonnet is advantageous to fair or rosy complexions; it may be trimmed with white flowers, but preferably with rose. A rose-colored bonnet must not be too close to the skin; if it is found that the hair does not produce sufficient separation, the distance from the rose-color may be increased by means of white or green, which is preferable . . . A yellow bonnet suits a brunette very well, and receives with advantage violet or blue accessories; the hair must always interpose between the complexion and headdress. It is the same with bonnets of an orange color . . . A blue bonnet is only suitable to a fair or bright red complexion . . . A violet bonnet is always unsuitable to every complexion."

* * *

"A young lady who lately gave an order to a milliner for a bonnet, said: — 'You are to make it plain, but at the same time smart, as I sit in a conspicuous place in church.'"

"We know nothing so revolting to the sense of grave people of both sexes as was the first use among us of ladies' *pantalettes*, which came into use slowly and cautiously about the year 1830. We well remember the first female who had the hardihood to appear abroad in their display; she was a tall girl in her minority, always accompanied by her mother, the wife of a British officer, come then to settle among us. Her pantalettes were courageously displayed among us, with a half length petticoat. Often we heard the remark in serious circles, that it was an abomination unto the Lord to wear men's apparel. The fashion, however, went first for children till it got familiar to the eyes, and then ladies, little by little, followed after, till in time they became pretty general as a *'defence from cold in winter,'* and for — we know not what — *in summer!*"

"Cold water preserves the freshness of the skin, and prevents wrinkles and everything of that kind, to a great degree. Followed and preceded by friction, it is beyond all possible value. A person who bathes in cold water freely can hardly feel the fluctuations of the weather, or be liable to take cold, or receive any injury from atmospheric changes. She will rarely ever have a pain, or be liable to fever, to rheumatism, or inflammation of the lung, or pleurisy, or quinsy, or sore throat, or cough, or skin disease, liver complaints or dyspepsia."

* * *

"Daily exercise in the open air is absolutely indispensable to health and beauty. American ladies are not good walkers simply because they do not practice walking. Many confine themselves at home during the long winters, keeping close in their heated rooms. Of course, debility ensues, nervousness and loss of all bloom as well as sprightliness. The eye becomes dull, the step feeble or loitering, and when such inanimate beings go abroad, they appear to see nothing and care for nothing except to finish their task of walking and reach home . . . American girls, even Mrs. Trollope admits, are 'almost always pretty,' but they fade early in consequence of not taking proper care of themselves."

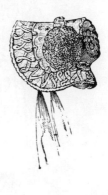

13

The Plain Straw Hat: "It refines the homeliest and composes the wildest; it gives the coquettish young lady a little dash of demureness, and the demure one a slight touch of coquetry; it makes the blooming beauty look more fresh, and the pale one more interesting; it makes the plain woman look, at all events, a lady, and the lady more lady-like still. A vulgar woman never puts on a straw bonnet . . . The genuine straw bonnet stamps the genuine American woman — no other country can produce either the hat or the wearer."

* * *

Misjudging the fickleness of the fashionable, John F. Watson, the famous chronicler of Philadelphia's history, expressed his relief at the demise of leg-of-mutton sleeves and full dresses in the thirties. The dresses but not the sleeves came back, fuller than ever in the forties, an age when ladies were clothed more heavily than they would be during the entire century: "They are gone, bag and baggage, and our belles are no longer compelled to walk the streets, as though suffering the penalties of justice, with eight or ten pounds of silk, chally, gros-de-something, muslin, merino, Circassian, Canton, crape barege, white satin, printed calico, or pelisse-cloth, dangling from each shoulder; or to exhibit themselves with a

pair of feather pillows stuck upon each side of their graceful figures, and far surpassing them in magnitude. The day of five feet high and six feet wide is gone, we trust, forever. . . ."

❊   ❊   ❊

"Furs are all the rage in Philadelphia this winter. Pelisses are trimmed round, and in some instances lined with light furs, ermine, squirrel, chinchilla, &c. Mantillas and scarfs are sometimes entirely lined or trimmed with fur, such as fitch blue, fox, martin, squirrel, or long white fur. Large pelerines of fur having two long ends descending in front with commodious arm-holes, are also much worn." And so it was during the forties, during the cold and damp Philadelphia winters. Charles Oakford, one of the city's largest milliners, advertised those furs shown below for the winter of 1847. Both are tippets, the one on the left in Parisian style, the other American.

❊   ❊   ❊

"If a lady sports a shawl at all, and none but very falling shoulders should venture, we should recommend it to be always falling off or putting on, which produces pretty action, or she should wear it up one shoulder and down the other, or in some way drawn irregularly, so as to break the uniformity. One of the faults of the present style

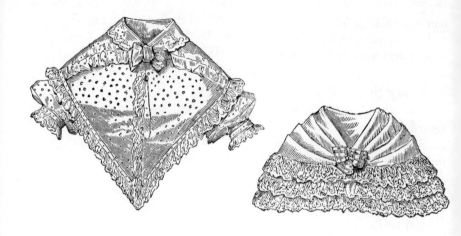

is, as every real artist knows, that it offers too few diagonal lines. The basque skirt is simply a deep ruffle, with edge of needlework Nothing is more picturesque than a line across the bust, like the broad ribbon of the garter across the graceful queen, or the loose girdle sloping to the hips, as in the costume of the early Plantagenets. On this very account, the long scarf shawl is as picturesque a thing as a lady can wear."

* * *

"Far be it from us to describe the mystery of the *berthe* — except as the cestus of Venus transferred from the Waist to the shoulders. We men have worn almost every part of a woman's dress, so that scarcely one sex has been known from the other; but, thank heaven, this, at all events, has remained sacred. No man ever wore a *berthe*."

* * *

"A Muff. — A thing that holds a young lady's hand without squeezing it."

* * *

"Some few of what are now-a-days called mantillas, which are the cardinals and capuchins of a century ago, are pleasing and blameless. A black velvet one turned up with a broad, dull black lace, like bright metal chased with lead, is very good. Also, when made of plain silk, black or light-colored, with no other trimmings than,

16

in milliner's language, 'the own.' But too often these articles, of which an endless variety exists, are merely made the vehicle for indulging a weakness for fringe, gimp, and other such trumpery."

* * *

"Fashion rules the world, and a most tyrannical mistress she is, compelling people to submit to the most inconvenient things imaginable, *for fashion's sake*. She pinches our feet with tight shoes, or chokes us with a tight neck-handkerchief, or squeezes the breath out of our body by tight lacing; she makes people sit up late by night when they ought to be in bed, and keeps them in bed in the morning when they ought to be up and doing. She makes it vulgar to wait upon one's self, and genteel to live idle and useless. She makes people visit when they would rather stay at home, eat when they are not hungry, and drink when they are not thirsty. She is a despot of the highest grade, full of intrigue and cunning, and yet husbands, wives, fathers, mothers, sons and daughters, servants, black and white, voluntarily have become her obedient servants and slaves, and vie with one another, to see who shall be the most obsequious!"

17

"Are there any who think this attention to the fashions of dress inconsistent with our lessons of morality? We hope not. We are sure those who reflect on this subject must become convinced it is important for the cause of moral and mental progress that the ladies who lead in the movement should show examples of order and taste in every department of female conduct. The woman who is careless and indifferent of her personal appearance loses half her influence. If we would have goodness show its greatest attraction, we must make it graceful."

* * *

Above are the Oakford spring fashions for 1849, from left to right are a Jenny Lind, a fine braid hat for girl's wear; a fine braid hat for boys, brim-supported for strength; and a traveling cap like a jockey.

* * *

To the right is an opera headdress from 1849. "The front hair divided in the centre of the forehead, then frizzed and arranged in full bandeaux on each side of the face. Across the upper part of the head is worn a wreath of foliage and flowers, descending very low at each side." The back view shows that "the back hair is tied a little below the crown of the head; then combed upwards, and a small cushion pinned on the head. The hair is next combed over the cushion, and brought down nearly to the nape of the neck, . . . The plaits are fixed round the head in a circular direction, one being turned to the right side, and the other to the left; the ends turned in and fastened at the lower part."

* * *

"Valuable Receipt. — to win affections of a maid — to fan a flame with a flirt — to corner a coquette — to get buttons sewed on your dickey every week — to cure a scolding wife — in short, to get two rays of home sunshine in the place of one, get 'Godey's Lady's Book.' "

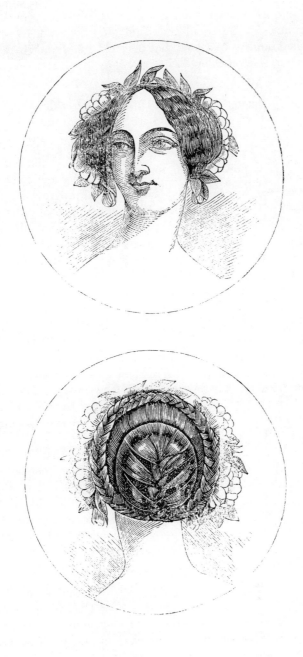

"A Lady, rather sentimental, inquired at a hat and cap store . . . for a cap of a 'subdued mouse-color.' The clerk replied, with all the composure he could command after so violent a shock, that they had none of that kind, but he could supply her with an article of 'an enraged rat-color.' "

* * *

Beauty is twin with Health, an ne'er deserts
Those maidens who are sedulous to pay
Due honors to her sister. Seek for Health,
And Beauty, ever in close neighborhood,
As flowers are fairest on the freshest stalk,
Will set her roses in your cheeks, and leave
Her diamond and pearls to make you fair.

Anon.

* * *

"Flounces are a nice question. We like them when they wave and flow, as in a very light material — muslin or gauze, or *barege* — when a lady has no outline and no mass, but looks like a receding angel or a 'dissolving view'; but we do not like them in a rich material where they float, or in a stiff one where they bristle, and where they break the flowing lines of the petticoat and throw light and shade where you don't expect them. In short, we like the gown that can do without flounces, as Josephine liked a face that could do without whiskers, but in either case it must be a good one."

* * *

"Economy is not limited to avoiding extravagance. It will induce you to purchase the most substantial and durable materials for your dress. For example, to buy a straw hat instead of a silk one, a calico instead of a silk one, a calico instead of a muslin gown, &c. Economy will teach you to mend up an old gown, and make it do, instead of buying a new one."

* * *

The forties ended much the same as the preceding fragment, with domestic frugality paramount and frivolity at ebb. But those who wanted for that virtue pushed the effects of dress to ridiculous extremes, extremes which would reach extravagant proportions by the early fifties.

N THE FIFTIES the woman of the home left and emerged into the public eye. She fought in temperance movements for the sobriety she saw in her sex. No longer was morality sought for only at home; the poor, the suffering animal, the sick, and the over-worked were in need of aid. The Bloomer, that ridiculous fad, died suddenly, but its significance as a symbol of woman's rights did not. Cinderella tales like *Jane Eyre* caught the imaginations of the ladies. *Moby Dick, Uncle Tom's Cabin,* and *The Scarlet Letter* had just been published. It was a partially liberated age.

Sewing machines were to be had for work at home, in part inspiring the extravagance of the dress of the age. Crafts were practiced by all those at home, among them crocheted and knitted flowers, bugle and bead work, shell work, painting on glass, hair work, drawing, and feather craft.

As much as twenty to twenty-five yards of cloth was used on a dress and, by the end of the century, as much as one hundred and fifty yards of material for flouncing found its way onto the over-burdened woman. Petticoats grew some more and were stiffer than ever; hoops aided in puffing out the gowns, as did wired petticoats, the artificial crinoline. Many women burned to death with under-clothes aflame. Hats and bonnets became miniscule, bodices tighter, sleeves wider. The sleeves, in fact, made hands appear almost non-existent, with their huge puffed undersleeves, beautifully embroidered, growing almost daily. Velvets and silks were common for morning and evening. The shape of a woman became triangular.

21

On the page opposite is a "Robe de Nuit," a nightgown advertised as one of the newest styles in 1851. It is made "of linen cambric and Valenciennes lace, and is intended for a *trousseau*. It may, however, be made very prettily of any style of plain cambric or muslin, with less expensive edging." Below is an article from the same year called a *matinée*, and intended to be thrown on in the early part of the morning, and worn during breakfast. It is composed of jaconet or mull muslin, and is trimmed with frills of needlework. "The make is similar to that of the ordinary lace muslin pardessus . . . It opens in a point in front, and is fastened at the waist by a bow

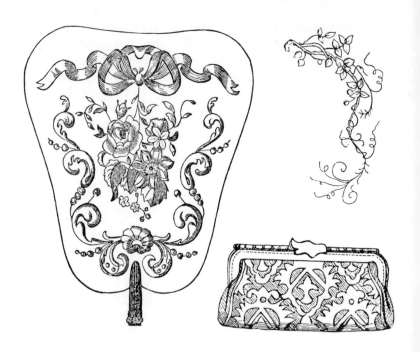

of blue satin ribbon with long ends. The *matinée* is finished at the
bottom with a full flounce of muslin cut out in small vandykes and
edged with buttonhole stitch or braid. Above this edge there is a
double row of braid or satin stitch, . . . A plain row of this frilling,
set on with the points inwards, trims the two fronts and the neck.
The sleeves, . . . are edged with a frill like that at the bottom of the
matinée, and are gathered up at the inside of the arm by bows of
blue ribbon with long ends. Attached to the back of the neck is the
hood, edged with a vandyked frill, and drawn by a blue ribbon tied
by a bow in front. The hood is intended either to fall back or to be
drawn over the head, serving as a cap at pleasure."

❀ ❀ ❀

Early in the fifties embroidered screens enjoyed a new vogue.
Working up one was often a part of the idle-hour diversion of many
a young miss. The one above is typical of the patterns, using white
satin as the ground and silk for the embroidery. The back is finished
in a contrasting silk. After the needlework was finished, the whole
was stretched over a frame, bound by tape, and edged with braid or

24

cord. For those less proficient, muslin and wool were suggested. The design to the right of the fan is for an handkerchief corner. The usual motif was white silk on white cambric. Below it is a purse of applique crimson velvet on leather — "a very pretty gift from a gentleman to a lady."

* * *

Pictured below are two dresses for little girls, both rather elaborate and meant for formal occasions, from the summer of 1852. The first is for a girl three or four years old, "of white cambric, the front of

the skirt *en tablier,* or apron fashion, . . . The waist and sleeves are in the same style." The second is "tucked India or Nansook muslin. The tucks upon the skirt form the heading to two deep scolloped ruffles. The waist has a slight *basque,* also tucked and ruffled, and the sleeves correspond."

"We give these as late and graceful fashions; but, nevertheless, recalling our first nursery rule to the attention of young mothers — the more simply a child is dressed, as a general thing, the better the

effect." The children's robes shown above, however, are drastically
more practicable. The first is of muslin and plain except for the
tucks. It is meant for a child old enough to be shown to company,
though the editor advises against the practice unless the visitors
ask expressly "to *see* the little innocent." The other is also of muslin
but slightly more decorative in the embroidered sleeves.

✻ ✻ ✻

The oppressive Philadelphia summers constantly depressed the
women of fashion. Only the fabrics relieved them. The robe
pictured opposite is especially for the torrid August weather. It
is "of white cambric muslin; and intended to be worn with a fine
under skirt, as it is open in front. The two front breadths are ornamented with embroidery in a rich and elegant arabesque design.
The corsage is without a collar, and scalloped to correspond to the
skirt. A plain lace chemisette is, of course, intended to be worn
beneath. The sleeves, which are demi-long, may be worn with or
without undersleeves."

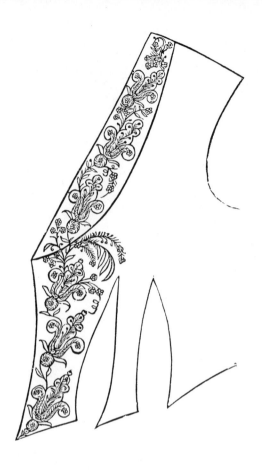

The popularity of embroidered vests lasted throughout most of the nineteenth century and was embraced by both men and women alike. Above is one of the typical patterns illustrated during the years of *Godey's* fashion reign. The cut-out effect is a simulated pattern for a third of the vest, the back being the unworked part, of course. In this example the materials are blue satin and embroidery silk of the desired colors. For a less expensive construction, muslin and lace were suggested. The buttons were to be of gold, set with turquoise. This particular style was one of the new fashions for the summer of 1852.

❋　❋　❋

On the opposite page, upper left, is the "Gilet," a newly introduced jacket for the wardrobes of "our fair country women. They

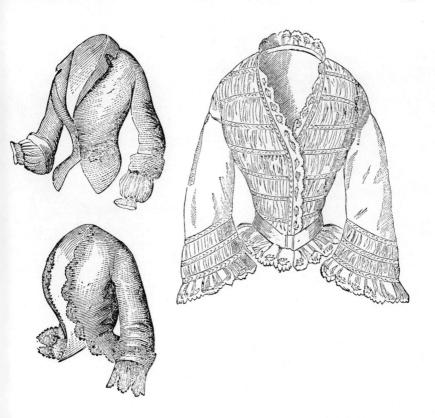

are most suitable for a promenade toilet, though, when made of a light or rich material, dinner dresses are improved by them." The upper example is of white Marseilles, "and intended to be worn with a plaid silk or poplin skirt. It has a rolling collar, and is ornamented with small enamelled buttons. The sleeves are *en revers,* or turned over so as to form a cuff." The second is of watered silk, "a deep *Marie Louise* blue. Instead of the collar, it has an edge of needle work, the scollops being very deep. The gilet is lined with white silk, and the entire corsage is open in front, intended to display a costly chemisette." To the right is the *canezou,* a blouse. Corsages varied on them depending on the style; some were high, others low. This particular one is of Swiss muslin and is "intended for a dinner or evening dress for a small company. It may be worn with a white muslin or light silk skirt. The body is composed of alternate rows of fine Swiss insertion and puffings, or, as the French call them, *borrillonnées,* of plain muslin made very full. The sleeves are plain to the elbow, where they widen trumpet-shaped, and are finished

in the same style as the corsage, edged by a wide row of embroidery. The same also surrounds the throat and edges the corsage which is clasped by a belt . . . and a buckle of pearl, gold, or enamel."

✳ ✳ ✳

A favorite bonnet for the spring of 1853, the side view indicates "a casing of straw-colored silk, edged with gauze ribbon on every division — thus giving a light and graceful contrast. Outside, it is quite plain, having only a full bow of the same shade of ribbon at the right. Full-blown blush roses, mixed with *thulle,* inside the brim." The front view presents "the brim of a bonnet in which the trimming, a wreath of field daisies, encircles the face. At the sides, it is merged into a bouquet of May-roses and foliage. The edge of the brim is of fine pointed blonde."

✳ ✳ ✳

"The Lady. — The aim of a real lady is always to be natural and unaffected, and to wear her talents, her accomplishments, and her

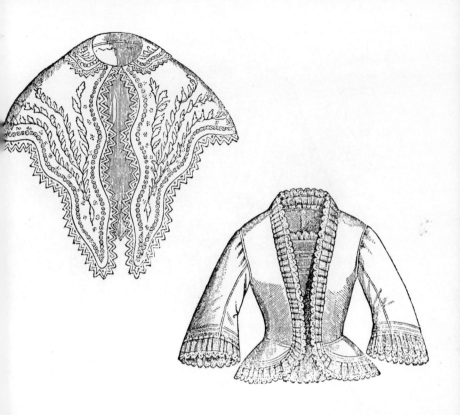

learning, as well as her newest and finest dresses, as if she did not know she had them about her."

*　*　*

"As many ladies who, for convenience or lightness of dress, wear low corsages in the evening, do not like to leave the neck entirely exposed, we give a new style, . . . of pelerine, . . . the edges waved or scalloped, so as to give a glimpse of the figure from the throat to the waist. There is a very pretty style edged with Valenciennes instead of the worked points. The collar to be fastened by a knot of some bright-colored satin ribbon, . . ." The second spring style is a cambric basque, "intended for a breakfast dress, with some pretty skirt. It will be found a convenient fashion to use up those that have had the waists condemned as too much worn. It is made quite plainly, with edges and chemisette of cambric flouncing, and may be sent to the common wash."

"Cleaning Black Lace. — Wash it in skimmed milk, do not rub, but constantly squeeze it softly. When it seems clean, take it out, and put it into a little clean milk, also skimmed; give it another squeeze, and lay it out directly on sheets of stout paper . . . If laid on anything soft, the moisture is absorbed, and the lace will not be so new looking."

❀ ❀ ❀

The figure above is a cambric basque, "or sacque, to be worn with [an] ornamented skirt . . . or a plainer one. It is in two shirrs, or drawings, on the shoulder, and has corresponding ones near the belt. The basque skirt is simply a deep ruffle, with edge of needlework embroidery in points. A triple ruffle of the same surrounds the neck and sleeves, where it is headed by three narrow tucks."

❀ ❀ ❀

"The question is: Do women dress to please themselves? Do they dress to please each other? Or, do they dress to please the men? A cynical bachelor says: 'They dress to worry other women.' "

32

"Now that the warm weather makes the question of low-cut dresses and short sleeves practicable, we have selected a cape, or rather pointed *berthé*, and canezou, that will be suitable to be worn with either lawns, *barèges*, silks, or organdies." The first of the styles, shown below, is "an extended *berthé*, intended for a plain low corsage. There is a puffing of embroidered muslin, with a narrow edge surrounding the neck, and two rows of muslin flouncing in a star pattern, making a point extending to the bottom or belt of the corsage. Flat bows of some delicate-hued Mantua ribbon, ending in points, decorate the front." The other, a canezou of French muslin, is "in basque form, without sleeves, the sides and large collar trimmed with muslin flouncing. Two bows and ends of some rich ribbon fasten it in front. This will be found very elegant and tasteful."

* * *

A Boston professor, in one of the issues of *Godey's*, wrote the editors praising the fashionable women of Philadelphia by saying: "The dress of the ladies is very rich — more rich than glaring with colors. One can tell a Philadelphia lady anywhere by the perfect taste — that art which conceals art — that agreeable harmony that pervades her whole costume, from ribbon of her hat to the color of her glove or gaiter boot. The same tone is kept through all."

* * *

Early in the fifties, cosmetics came under attack by physicians and pharmacologists. White paint, usually a lead compound, had

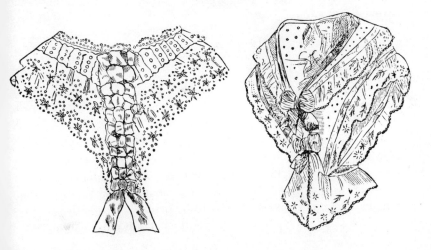

caused eruptions, dizziness, and blindness in some isolated cases. Those who indulged in the vain practice of lining their eyes or using cosmetics were warned frequently about the physical as well as the moral dangers of the practice. The usual advice was to refrain from using unnatural means to accomplish the blush, fragrant look of youth, and correction of nature's faults, and to use the best cosmetic: early hours, exercise, and cleanliness.

* * *

Above is a typical child's fashion of the mid-fifties. In almost every case the fashions of the children were a reflection of those of the adults. In this case, the length of the skirt and the style of under-garment are the main differences. The flouncing on the skirt, the bonnet, the bodice, and sleeves basically parallel those of the grown-ups. The stance is typical, indicating the child at play. Throughout

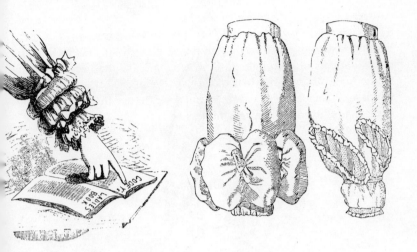

the century physicians frequently advised *Godey's* readers on the practice of clothing children, some contending that they should be protected from the elements at all times, even in the warmest weather, others taking the position that children were overclothed, as indeed they were. It was a difficult issue to resolve, especially because the adults themselves did not normally dress comfortably or wisely.

* * *

Pictured is a knitted lace undersleeve, intended to be made by those who do such work at home. Its ruffle extends only to the top of the hand, as is fashionable, and not falling over. Two other styles of undersleeve are shown, detached from the chemisettes which they match. Both are demi-long and are intended to fasten "neatly above the elbow by a hook or button, and allowing an easy fulness for the puff below."

* * *

"To Clean White Satin Shoes. — Put in the shoe something which will fill it out. Then rub the shoe gently with a piece of muslin dipped in spirits of wine. Do this several times. Then wipe the shoe carefully with a piece of dry muslin."

* * *

Lamenting the black and white illustration for the latest slippers of 1855, the editor tempted the ladies of fashion by stating: "If we were able to present in the rich colors and metallic lustres of the

velvets and chenilles of the originals, we fear would almost tempt our friends to infringe upon the tenth commandment. These slippers are made of various colored velvets . . . with delicately quilted linings of primrose taffeta; a quilling of satin ribbon trims the tops; the quarters are exquisitely embroidered with natural tinted flowers, wrought with chenille."

❋ ❋ ❋

"A Woman Of Good Taste. — You see this lady turning a cold eye to the assurances of shopmen and the recommendation of milliners. She cares not how original a pattern may be, if it be ugly, or how recent a shape, if it be awkward. Whatever laws fashion dictates, she follows a law of her own, and is never behind it. She wears very beautiful things which people generally believe to be fetched from Paris, or at least made by a French milliner, but which as often are bought at the nearest town and made up by her maid. Not that her costume is either rich or new; on the contrary, she wears many a cheap dress, but it is always good . . . After all, there is no great art either in her fashions or her materials. The secret simply consists in her knowledge, the grand unities of dress — her own station, her own age, and her own points. And no woman can dress well who does not." So said L. A. Godey, the publisher of "The Book," despite the indications the magazine often gave to the contrary.

36

The cap below is a "dress cap for an invalid. Fauchon of rose-colored silk, bordered with three rows of black velvet ribbon, and edged by a row of medium black guipure. This has the effect of a half-handkerchief of silk thrown lightly over a cap composed of three quillings of plain blonde. Bows and strings of pale rose-colored ribbon."

*　*　*

"Frank, where have you been? You are in a perfect glow."
　"I've been playing an old game — *chasing a hoop* in Chestnut Street."

*　*　*

Crinolines became more and more of a nuisance to those who wore them and especially to those who didn't. In New York, as in any large city, these billowing skirts forced men into the street, crowded people in stores, and caused a commotion on the omnibuses of the cities. In an attempt to combat the inconvenience caused to other customers of the street car lines, the New York omnibus company raised the fare appropriately: "Ladies with Hoops, 12 cents."

"The Bloomer costume has not been so successful in [England] as some of its warm American friends seemed to anticipate . . . It was rather fatal to the new dress that a Bloomer should have been burnt in effigy on Guy Fawkes' Day."

❀ ❀ ❀

The same correspondent wrote later from London: "We had enough of Bloomers here of late. They serve at the bars of public houses, dressed in pants, straw hats, and ostrich feathers; also in the cigar and coffee shops — the sign-board being, 'A genuine Bloomer serves constantly here.' "

❀ ❀ ❀

One of the more stylish and elaborate mantles in vogue during the spring of 1855 was the "Antoinette," illustrated above. It was meant to be worn as a "step between a cloak and the lighter summer scarfs, . . . It is in three parts; a double pelerine; the first rounding on the shoulders; the second falling just below the waist, with a full basque or flounce attached." The material was dark green peau de soie and the "trimming a broad band of Tartan taffeta ribbon."

The dress is a fancy frock for children's dress parties. "The skirt is of white cashmere, with a deep border of ruby-colored velvet, . . . Peasant's bodice, of ruby velvet, over a waist and sleeves of white Swiss muslin, carelessly laced and tied by ribbons to correspond."

* * *

"There is another foolish and pernicious fashion we have also warned mothers to avoid — that of dressing little children in low-necked frocks. Boys are exempted from this display of their fair shoulders at an early age, but little girls are, by the absurd and, we must use plain language, wicked vanity of their mother, often subjected to such an uncomfortable as well as injurious mode of dress, till their forms are permanently injured."

* * *

"To raise the pile of velvet, hold it over a basin of boiling water, the wrong side of the velvet being next to the water."

* * *

On the following page is an example of a "set," a chemisette and detachable sleeves, the sleeves illustrated earlier in this chapter,

40

examples of the varieties of styles that might be had by using various combinations. The parts are tacked together and disassembled before cleaning. At left is a mantle of cambric embroidery, intended for watering places, the morning, or a hotel. It is meant to be worn in lieu of a cloak. The child's frock is of broad bands of English embroidery on white cambric. It is intended for party wear or dinner, without the sleeves which are secured by elastic bands for easy removal. The trimming is blue satin ribbon with flowing ends, and the ensemble is finished with a version of the popular chip hat trimmed with white satin ribbon and a light or contrasting plume on the right side. It is intended for spring.

"I saw five brave maids, sitting on five broad beds, braiding broad braids. I said to those five brave maids, sitting on five broad beds, braiding broad braids: Braid broad braids, brave maids." Say three times quickly.

❋ ❋ ❋

On the opposite page is a lady's netted purse of fine mesh, darned with gold, green and white. Below it is the "Marion," a cloak of velvet. "It is extremely youthful in shape, and trimmed with broad velvet, satin, or galloon of a running pattern." The companion cape, the "Nightingale," "is of moire and lace, violet or black. A broad band or yoke of the silk forms a shoulder piece on which is set a flounce of black lace in easy fullness. Below this comes a flounce of the silk put on in square, hollow plaits, which is in turn followed by lace set on a net foundation."

"We agree . . . that the care of the nails adds greatly to the beauty of the hand. The nails should be well brushed with soap and water, and when quite dry, with lemon-juice, to be washed off again with clean water. Pare back the scarf skin at the root, but never cut it, or you will have nail springs, . . . an untidy, and sometimes very uncomfortable appendage. . . ."

❉   ❉   ❉

"Eccentricity in dress belongs only to two classes of society, the very high or the very low. The *real lady is always the partisan of simplicity,* by which we mean the absence of everything, in color and ornament, so showy as to offend the purest taste."

❉   ❉   ❉

"At this time a fashionable dry goods store advertises, a lace scarf for 1500 dollars!" John Watson commented in 1856. "Another, has a bridal dress for 1,200 dollars — Bonnets at 200 dollars are also sold. Cashmeres, from 300 dollars and upwards, are seen by dozens along Broadway. And 100 dollars is quite a common price for a silk gown. Think of such a sale of prices for 'un-ideaed' American women! Can the pampering of such vanities, elevate the character of our women? Alas! the women who live for such displays — who give their whole attention to diamonds and dress, are fast becoming

44

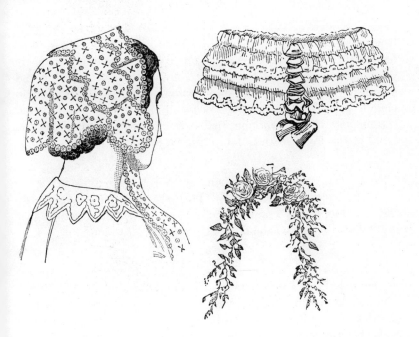

unfitted for wives or mothers — and are operating the ruin of husbands and parents. — "

* * *

The article on the opposite page is a bretelle with a body and sleeves of blonde, velvet ribbon, and black lace. It is meant to be worn with an evening dress which is cut low. Above is a fauchon, or half-handkerchief cap, decorated with English embroidery. It has scalloped edges and rounded corners, the ribbon effect crossing it of English embroidery. The bertha is of lace headed by tulle. The ribbon should fall with bows and a flowing end to be tasteful. The garland for the back of the hair can be made of natural, knitted, or paper flowers. It is meant to encircle braids at the back of and fall low on the neck.

* * *

John Watson, in his *Annals*, commented very little on fashion in Philadelphia, but when he did, it came in the usual way — as moral, righteous, attack. So with "Hoops Again!": "We had hoped that our ladies would never again be brought to use such ill-looking, useless and deforming appendages to their dresses — They are, as seen along our streets, a Misdemeanor. They are so suggestive of im-

45

modest thoughts, both while worn and also when seen dangling from stores along the streets, just like so many paraschutes. One feels as if they must be scanning them, to conjecture how and where the limbs therein could be found! They are too, so annoying and engrossing of place and room in omnibuses — Rail cars, and in church pews and aisles — and *why* all this; but as spell bound *subserviants* to some *foreign* spell — one feels scandalized for 'the Land of the Free!' " Speak for your own thoughts, John.

✿ ✿ ✿

"George, you are looking very smiling. What has happened?"

"The most delightful thing. I caught my Jenny by surprise, this morning, in her wrapper, and *without hoops;* and I got the first kiss I've had since whalebone skirts came into fashion."

✿ ✿ ✿

Crinolines weren't all bad. One was an ally of poor dumb animals. A young lady of San Francisco went out for the air, taking her "Poopsy," a gay little terrier, with her for company. She knew that the dog was unlicensed, but didn't care. "Poopsy" had needed a walk, license or not, so out they went. Before she had blushed at a dozen men, the "catchers" arrived, having been informed by some upright citizen only a little before, of a "fast woman" walking a "lawless" dog. A crowd following behind, they approached, hoping

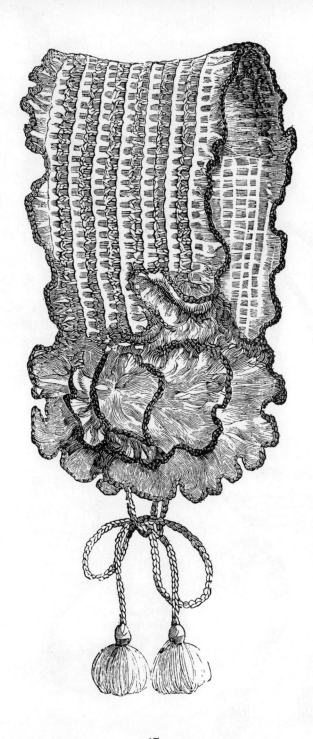

47

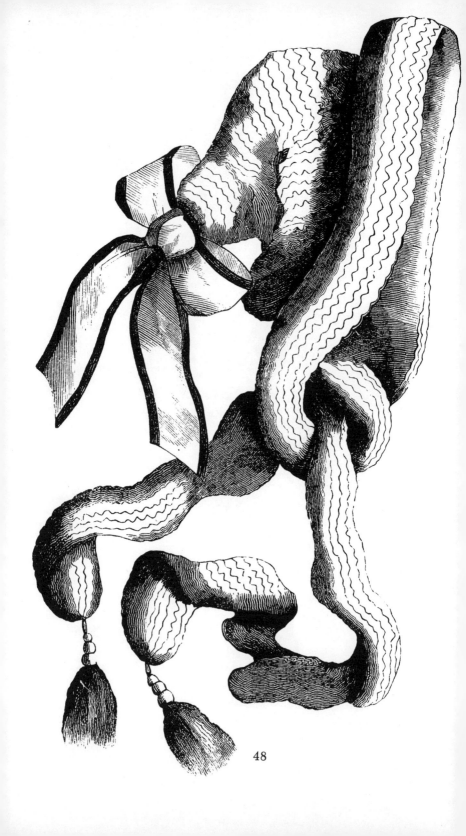

48

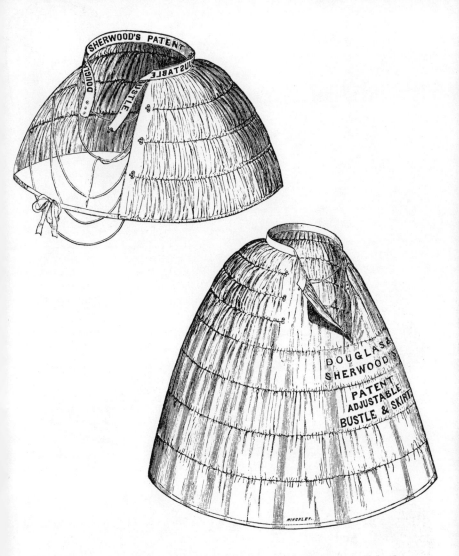

to tear the poor pup from his dear mistress. She cast a small look at the fiends, modestly lifted her crinoline slightly. The pup scurried underneath; the crowd cheered and applauded; and with some consternation, the "catchers," shrugging, went on their way, defeated by the crinoline.

* * *

Opposite is a knit opera hood. It is made of blue or pink wool, contrasting ribbon done in a large bow. For the winter of 1856–1857 the fashion was both stylish and comfortable.

On the page previous is *Douglas & Sherwood's* "Patent Adjustable Bustle And Skirt": "The high estimation in which these articles are held by the ladies, and the recommendations of many distinguished physicians, induce us to give our voice also in their favor. Combining lightness with extreme elasticity and strength, they give a graceful contour to the form, relieve the spine from the heat caused by wearing a great number of thicknesses, and thus obviate the evils of compressing the figure, the prolific source of such terrible maladies. They are made of fine cloth. The Bustle is of round whalebone, extending part of the way round the skirt; at their ends are eyelets, through which a corset lace is passed. Observe that this is laced across, or over the back, not round the person. By simply drawing

the lace, the size of the bustle may be increased at pleasure . . . The second engraving is the Bustle, with the skirt added — in one garment. It has steel springs of superior quality, with a cord at the bottom."

*   *   *

The skirt at the left opposite is a woven extension skirt, of steel springs and taped weaving. It serves the same function as the crinoline, but is less warm and bulky. Next to it is the "Self-Supporting Tournure": "That this invention should have been made long ago, is surprising, for it is very simple, and yet the very best article to give beauty to the human figure. All other devices to give rotundity to the shape betray themselves, while this yields to the figure and makes no sign of its existence in the gait of a lady. The light, pliant steel springs which proceed from the steel waistband — below or above the edge of it, as may be needed by short or long waists, perform their office admirably. These are represented by the vertical bands. The horizontal ones represent broad tapes, which sustain the general drapery. Nothing could be invented so well calculated to meet the demands of those who, in full dress, wish to present the realization of a well shaped and graceful figure. This Tournure is now generally adopted by fashionable ladies in all parts

of the country, and is prized because it never loses its ability to sustain and round the skirts, without suggesting that it is employed for such a purpose . . . Ladies will be delighted to throw away the cumbersome articles hitherto used to improve the figure, and adopt this admirable invention, which has been patented."

* * *

On the preceding page is the juvenile fashion, "La Belle Petite," a "dress of plaid poplin, in large bars, blue and white. A jacket corsage, trimmed with three rows of *Tom Ponce* fringe, blue and white. Street basque of light ladies' cloth, with grelots; the sleeves

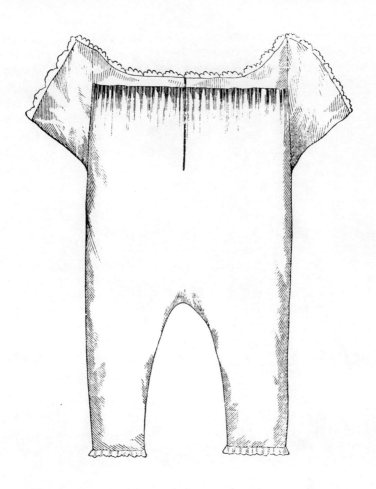

are open to the band of the arm. Undersleeves and collar of muslin. Leghorn hat, with blue ribbons."

* * *

A cap and bonnet from the late fifties: the first is of plaid uncut velvet, blue and white. The other is also for spring and is of white split straw with a narrow blonde fall and a wreath of daisies about the crown.

* * *

Above is the "Nonpareil Garment." "This garment, combining the chemise and drawers, has very many advantages. We recommend

it especially to ladies travelling, to those giving out their wash, and to ladies boarding. It is also decidedly cooler for summer."

* * *

Above is the celebrated *Douglas & Sherwood's* Tournure Corset; opposite is the back view. There were so many attacks against corseting that almost any issue of *Godey's* contained either an attack

or a defense on the controversy. Among the non-medical attacks is
related by Lady Mary Wortley Montague: "One of the highest
entertainments in Turkey is having you go to their baths. When I
was first introduced to one, the lady of the house came to undress
me — another high compliment they pay to strangers. After she
slipped off my gown and saw my stays, she was very much struck

by the sight of them and cried out to the ladies in the bath, 'Come hither, and see how cruelly the poor English ladies are used by their husbands. You need not boast, indeed, of the superior liberties allowed you when they lock you up thus in a box!' "

*　*　*

Firescreens and fans of feathers were a perennial favorite. The one illustrated is of pheasant wings and is capable of being constructed at home: "Fire screens composed of the wings of pheasant, or other game, are both pretty and useful . . . The wings must be cut off when the bird is fresh killed, and as near the body as possible; being careful not to ruffle the feathers . . . When sewed, lay the screen on a table right side downwards, and, having placed a double paper over the sewing, press it with a hot iron. When that side is done,

turn the screen, and place a weight on the right side to give it a flat back; it then fits to attach to the handle, a gilt one looks best; form rosettes of the large scarlet chenille, and sew on each side so as to cover where the handle joins; a pair of scarlet chenille tassels and silk cord are required, as seen in [the] design. The screen is hung by the loop of cord."

✻ ✻ ✻

Above are examples of two summer slippers and a detachable sleeve for a chemisette. The first slipper is a quilted blue satin; the other is in bronze kid, with an applique pattern in blue silk and chain-stitch. The sleeve has two puffs of white muslin and a flounce of embroidery edged in lace, as is the collar. It is caught up at the forearm with a bow of some delicately shaded ribbon.

"Cold Cream. — White wax two drachms; spermaceti half an ounce; oil of sweet almonds two ounces — melt them over a slow fire; then, as it cools, whip or beat well in with a spoon two ounces of rose water, adding any scent you please."

*　*　*

"The robe is chosen for the season, [the summer], an exquisitely wrought French muslin, with double skirt; . . . A shock of broad blue ribbon confines at the waist." It is intended for the morning toilette and can be worn with either of the slippers illustrated on the previous page.

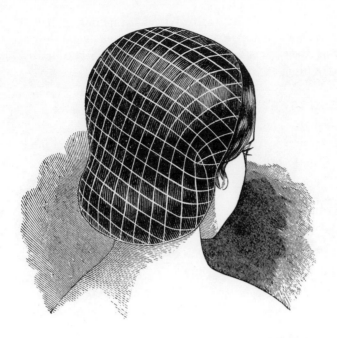

The popular hairnet above is a creation of silk braid, chenille, and "plain twist." It is meant to be fashioned at home. "Beads can be added if desired; but the net looks in better taste without."

* * *

"Fine Lavender Water. — Mix together, in a clean bottle, a pint of inodorous spirits of wine; an ounce of oil of lavender; a teaspoon of oil bergamot; and a tablespoon of the oil of ambergris."

* * *

On the following page is a child's shirt, intended for warm weather and to be worn without an over jacket. The fabric is linen or brillante. The handkerchief is for morning habit, as is the cap. It is cambric with "a deep hem and a single richly-wrought corner, a convolvulus, with leaves and tendrils." The cap has blue ribbon ties and bows and is of cambric or silk and fine needlework.

* * *

"Rose-red cannot be put in contrast with even the rosiest complexions without causing them to lose some of their freshness. Rose-red, maroon, and light crimson have the serious disadvantage of render-

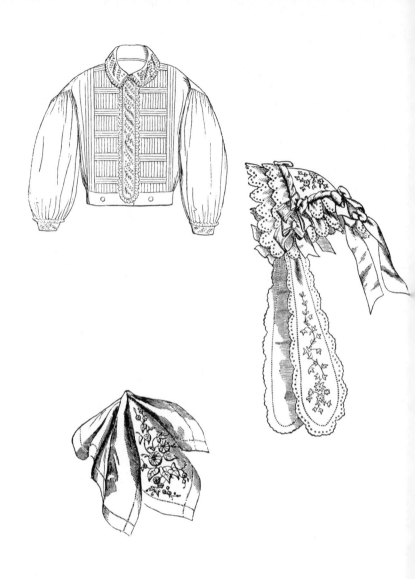

ing the complexion more or less green. It is necessary, then to separate the rose from the skin, in some manner; and the simplest manner of doing this is to edge the draperie with a border of thulle . . . Delicate green is, on the contrary, favorable to all fair complexions . . . Yellow imparts violet to a fair skin . . . To brunettes, on the contrary, it is becoming . . . Blue imparts orange, which combines favorably with white, and the light flesh tints of fair complexions . . . It will not suit brunettes . . . Orange is too brilliant to be elegant."

Illustrated here is a dress of the "sort of body worn by young ladies of between six and ten years of age. It is made of either spotted or sprigged muslin, and trimmed round with a double row of either lace or rich embroidery. This is worn over either a silk or colored muslin, and is confined round the waist with a rich ornamental silk cord and tassels, to match the under dress, which is made without a body. This article of dress is peculiarly French. It is light, elegant, and extremely convenient, as it can be worn over any variety of skirt, and at once converts whatever it thus accompanies into a costume suitable for all occasions."

Two warm weather children's outfits: the boy's has trousers of "nankeen, or white, or buff jean, with a needlework embroidery, in white, following the seams and waistband. The little waist or shirt is composed of alternate rows of white cambric puffs and inserting; a narrow edge of work around the neck and sleeves." The girl's is a "tunic dress, very much worn, and especially suited to the coming fall and winter season, when made in heavy materials. It consists of a skirt, shirt like that [on page 68], and a loose jacket with open sleeves; the scarf may or may not be worn about the waist. Scotch hat in Leghorn, with a plume. Needle-worked trowsers."

* * *

The hood opposite is intended for winter wear or a sea voyage. It is "of dark brown, green, or blue silk; the upper point or fauchon, the

curtain and the brim, trimmed with quilling of ribbon the same shade. It is becoming as well as serviceable shape, and the short, round corners make it decidedly new."

* * *

The cape on the following page is the "Saragossa." It is one of a "variety of modes made from the same general materials, characterized by the hood and trimming, which are so greatly admired. Some are shawl-shaped. The material employed in their construction are pine-apple cloths, mohair fabric, etc.; they are all trimmed with a quilling of the same. This new style of quilling made by indenting a groove longitudinally through the fluting near the edges, adds

much beauty to the garment, and with tassels forms the ornament of the burnous."

❋ ❋ ❋

A number of recipes for sweetening the breath are to be found in *Godey's*. Among them is the "Elixir of Roses":

"Cloves .... 12 grains
Cinnamon .... 40 grains
Ginger .... 3 drachms
Spirit of wine .... 1 pint
Oil of orange-peel .... 12 drops
Otto of roses .... 3 drops
Essence of peppermint .... 1½ drachms

These are to be mixed and allowed to soak for a fortnight. Then the liquor is to be filtered off for use. A small quantity is to be used to wash out the mouth in about as much water as is preferred."

❋ ❋ ❋

By the end of the fifties a woman's gowns were extravagant, as were the crinolines. She had discovered a kind of Cinderella dream in being partially liberated from the home and exercising her will in the real world. In the new decade, however, she would face more basic problems: finding a husband and clothing herself despite the high cost of living.

HAT COULD BE EXPECTED during the sixties? The Civil War spent half the decade as well as many of the men; Lincoln's assassination shocked the country. *Little Women* was published; the typewriter was invented; modern shoe manufacturing began. Men were scarce for the marriage-minded lady, a woman in her mid-twenties almost surely becoming a spinster. The cost of living rose and with it the style of living. There were leisurely lives for a few, luxurious and bored. The boredom led to a new leisure-time pursuit for some women in the form of sports like riding, croquet, and billiards. They had tasted liberation in the fifties and found it souring. The extremists were "fast," painted with cosmetics, false hair, dyed hair, and showing their ankles. To attract the men the colors became brighter, the skirts shorter and looped up, and the petticoats frilly.

In the South fashion somewhat lagged, the major reason being the war's isolation. Fashion monthlies were no longer readily available; fabrics were expensive. In fact, to one well-known lady of fiction it was a major discomfort of the war; Scarlett O'Hara missed her *Godey's Lady Book,* and said so.

The crinoline gave way to the looped-up skirt. That edged into a bustle or dress-improver. Garibaldi blouses and Zouave jackets became a vogue; the waterfall was a popular coiffure. Corsets came into greater vogue. Women were curvaceous.

Aprons became increasingly more popular in the sixties, especially as skirts became gored and the crinoline flat in front. On the previous page is the "Clementina" at top, and at bottom, the "Floria." Both are from the summer of 1860; the first is made of "silk, lace, narrow velvet, and buttons. The lace is inserted, and finished with the velvet ribbon, which is very effective and pretty." The second is shell shaped and described as "quite new. The ruffle is made of silk, . . . macaroons or rosette buttons finish each shell."

The article pictured on the opposite page is a glove top and is meant to be fastened directly to the glove or slipped over the cuff and held in place by elastic in the top itself. It is of black lace and black velvet ribbon.

❀ ❀ ❀

The fichu above is intended for summer wear and is particularly suited for evening or dinner dress. "It is quite graceful, and a newer shape than the favorite Marie Antoinette. The bows may be either of black velvet, or a shade of satin ribbon harmonizing with the dress."

The undersleeve above is intended for "summer dress where the flounce or sleeve is open to the jockey. It consists of a muslin puff, a deep flounce ornamented by rows of narrow violet ribbon, and edged a pretty pattern of embroidery, while another and smaller puff below, terminates in a ruff, held to the wrist by an elastic. Bow of broad velvet ribbon on the upper puff."

*　*　*

Opposite is a lady's short nightdress from September, 1860. This simple easy style is made of "rows of tucks and inserting down the front, and the sleeve is confined at the waist by a band of inserting, with a worked ruffle turned over on the sleeve. The collar is merely a band of inserting and a worked ruffle."

*　*　*

Complaints about the price of the Singer sewing machine, a mere $50, were often voiced in *Godey's*, but many preferred it over the popular Wheeler and Wilson. A gentleman wrote his thoughts on the best one, choosing both a more practicable labor saver and a less expensive one, he thought. "An Old Fashion Sewing-Machine" would cause no little turmoil today in some homes: "The very best sewing-machine a man can have is a wife. It is one that requires but a kind word to set it in motion, rarely gets out of repair, makes but little noise, will go uninterruptedly for hours, without the

slightest trimming, or the smallest personal supervision being necessary. It will make shirts, darn stockings, sew on buttons, mark
pocket handkerchiefs, cut out pinafores, and manufacture children's
frocks out of any old thing you may give it; and this it will do behind
your back just as well as before your face . . . Of course sewing
machines vary a great deal. Some are much quicker than others.
It depends, in vast measure, upon the particular pattern you select
. . . In short, no gentleman's establishment is complete without one."

❋ ❋ ❋

"Fire-Proof Dresses. — Scarcely a week passes but we read sad
accounts of young ladies being burnt to death, owing to their light
muslin garments catching fire. It ought to be generally known that
the light dresses may be made fire-proof at a mere nominal cost,

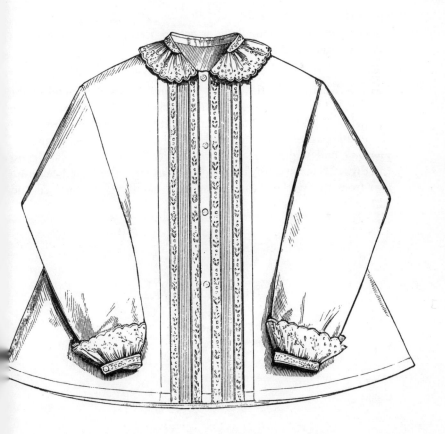

by steeping them, or the linen or cotton used in making them, in a dilute solution of chloride of zinc."

* * *

Caps and bonnets in the period between 1830 and the end of the century fall into three neat classes: those that were to be worn in the morning and in the house, those that were meant for dress, and those that were meant for night wear. Of the three types, the morning and night caps remained basically the same plain caps; the dress bonnets were the changing fashion. Illustrated here are two from the sixties, rather small half handkerchiefs of lace and ribbon or embroidery.

EDITOR'S NOTE: There has been no attempt to standardize the spelling, terminology, or punctuation in the descriptions of the fashions indicated by the color plates. They are as formerly described.

July 1831

Fig. 1. Dress of transparent crape over a white florence. Sleeves of blond or bobbinet, very wide and full, finished with cuffs and epaulettes of the same material as the dress. Hair in large folds and bows, with no other ornament than a white rose.

Fig. 2. Dress of painted muslin. Canezon handerkerchief of French worked muslin. Grenadine scarf. Bonnet, with a round crown of white gros de nap, and a front of coloured wood-lawn; folds of wood-lawn go nearly round the crown. The trimming is of white gauze riband, edged and figured with the same colour as the wood-lawn; each bow being finished with a knot at the bottom.

Fig. 3. The child's dress is a frock, pantalets and cape of cambric muslin, with a narrow border of coloured braiding. A straw hat.

October 1831

Fig. 1. Morning dress with a pelisse of lavender gray *gros de Naples, corsage en guimpe,* and sleeves *a la Medicis.* A *ruche* of the same material trims the *corsage en coeur* and descends in a perpendicular direction down the front of the skirt. The *collerette* is of white *tulle, capote de paque-bot*—it is of Leghorn straw, with a square brim lined with green satin. The crown is trimmed with three bands of green riband and a full cockade in the centre. The neck-knot is also of green riband. Black *gros de Naples brodequins.*

Fig. 2. Evening dress of Chinese green *gros de Naples;* corsage *a revers;* the *revers* is formed of dark green velvet. Sleeves *a la Medicis* with velvet cuffs. The trimming of the skirt consists of a velvet band, from which depend large leaves. The head dress is a white *gros de Naples* hat trimmed with rose coloured riband, and birds of Paradise plumes. The hair is dressed in full curls on the forehead, and in bows of moderate height on the summit of the head. A *chaperon* of roses and bluebells surround the base of the bows.

January 1835

Fig. 1. A coat dress of stone coloured silk. The capes trimmed with fur or silk, with buttons in front. Cashmere shawl with gay border. Green velvet bonnet, trimmed with gauze riband, or blond lace. In some instances the 'Bird of Paradise' is added to the trimming. Gaiters the same colour as coat.

Fig. 2. An evening dress. The under dress is *pou de soie,* the colour is white, slightly tinged with rose. The corsage is square, rises rather high in front, and is edged with narrow *blonde de Cambray.* The robe, a little shorter than the under dress, is composed of *taffetas de Siam,* the ground is a rich shade of golden brown, with a detached pattern delicately traced in green. *Corsage a l'Elizabeth* made tight to the shape, pointed in front; it is cut of the same height behind as the under dress, but much lower before. The trimming of the bust is *blonde de Cambray* set on narrow and almost plain on the bosom, but at its full width behind, forming a ruff in a lighter style than usual. A row of enamelled gold ornaments is placed perpendicularly on the *corsage,* and down the front of the under dress. The robe opens *en tablier* on each side. Short full sleeves, with *manchettes* corresponding with the lace on the bust. The hind hair is dressed very low, the front platted on each side, and the ends brought under a gold enamelled comb at the back of the head. The tiara, earrings, and neck-chain correspond. Necklace of large pearls. White lace gloves.

November 1841

Fig. 1. Black velvet dress, plain high corsage trimmed with a puff, as is also the sleeves, which are tight; the wrists finished with a cuff, which, as well as the sides of the sleeves, are trimmed with fancy silk buttons: the skirt is ornamented with a deep border of fur. Large mantilla shawl of velvet, trimmed with fur. Bonnet of fancy silk.

Fig. 2. A plain coloured mantle, made short enough to display the border of the dress. It is lined with cherry coloured satin, and trimmed with cherry cord. White silk Bonnet, inside ornamented with flowers, outside with feathers.

Fig. 3. Rich satin pelisse: skirt trimmed with fur, tight sleeves, finished with a fur cuff. Large fur cape. Hat trimmed with feathers.

Fig. 4. Child's dress of coloured velvet made loose, confined with a cord and tassel, and trimmed with fancy buttons up the front. Large cape, with cotton bonnet and feathers.

December 1842

Fig. 1. A long cloak of rich brown satin, trimmed with black velvet, finished with a deep fringe of twisted silk. A circular cape and collar of black velvet. Dress of blue gray peau de soie, made high in the neck, and worn with a pointed frill. Bonnet of the same material as the dress: the crown elevated. Feathers white, tipped with pale blue.

Fig. 2. Mantilla of sea green gros' Afrique, edged all round with points. Lapel front, terminating in a point at the waist. Dress trimmed with a double row of deep netting. Bonnet of white glacé silk, with a brown velvet trimming.

Fig. 3. A dress of nankeen-coloured gros de Suisse; trimmed down the front with ruches, meeting at the point of the corsage, and spreading out towards the hem at the bottom of the skirt. Cardinal or short cloak made very full, and trimmed all round with deep black lace. Bonnet of white corded silk; white feathers.

Fig. 4. Dress of light brown Thibet mousseline de laine. Cardinal of full blue satin lined with cinnamon coloured florence. Bonnet pale blue watered silk, with a ruche inside the brim.

February 1843

Fig. 1. A fashionable cloak, though not the handsomest worn this season. The material is a strong woollen cloth, not prepossessing in its appearance, but very durable and warm. Some of them have a small worked figure, which is a great relief. The size of the capes vary—many are longer than our pattern, and some shorter—we give the medium. The collar and cape are trimmed with a fringe of the same colour as the cloak.

Fig. 2. Is the latest French fashion, and has hardly yet got introduced among us. We received the first impression from our Paris correspondent in a letter, and we hastened to present it to our patrons. It is a graceful garment, and will be very popular. The material is merino. It is made to fit the figure, confined at the waist with a cord and tassel; Hungary sleeves; skirt short, trimmed with a cord and lined with fancy coloured silk. Bonnet trimmed with feathers.

Fig. 3. Blue velvet mantilla cloak, trimmed with swansdown— velvet hat and feathers.

Fig. 4. Silk dress, corsage high in the neck. It comes to a point at the waist, and is trimmed with pipings—a fanciful trimming down the sides of the skirt—a bonnet of shaded velvet, feather to correspond. It is now very fashionable to have the feather the same shade as the hat.

Fig. 5. Lavender silk coat dress, high in the neck—moderate sized cape, tight sleeves. The waist is finished with a narrow belt. White velvet bonnet and feathers.

May 1849

Fig. 1. Misses' dinner dress, or demi-toilette for the country. The dress itself, white jaconet, with four rows of embroidery upon the skirt. The corsage half high, and finished with a *tucker* of fine lace. Sleeves gathered at the wrist. A blue sash and hair ribbons.

Fig. 2. Small jacket, open and rounded in front, or dark velvet, cloth or cashmere, with buttons of the same. Small square linen collar turned over; a ribbon neck-tie. Loose trowsers of blue and white-striped linen. Cap of dark cloth.

Fig. 3. Dress of white lawn, a fall infant waist, and short sleeves; slip of pink French lawn, with the skirt as long as the dress, the waist made lower by an inch or two. Gaiters, and frilled panta-lettes showing a few inches. It will be noticed that the slip is tight behind, and is fastened by the bands and buttons in front— closed only at the bottom of the waist. Neat and useful aprons might be made in this style, having the skirt a little shorter than the dress.

Fig. 4. Coarse straw bonnet lined and trimmed with blue silk. White open-worked muslin waist, and a skirt of some light and delicate material. It may either be a *glace* silk, as in the plate, or lawn. French cambric, etc., etc., as best suits the mother's taste. Pantalettes quite plain, and finished by a narrow frill.

"Hair is at once the most delicate and lasting of our materials, and survives us like love. It is so light, so gentle, so escaping from the idea of death, that, with a lock of hair belonging to a child or friend, we may almost look up to heaven and compare notes with the angelic nature — may almost say: 'I have a piece of thee here, not unworthy of thy being now.' " Thus, read a frequent advertisement for hair ornaments, a fashion of the mid-fifties and later. One merely sent a lock of hair from a loved one or one lately departed and indicated one's preference, and it was transformed into a pin, watch fob, bracelet, ring, set of sleeve buttons, breast pins, brooches, or earrings. The price ranged from one dollar for a ring to fifteen for a larger item. Those pictured above are various types and are of early sixties vintage.

* * *

"The most healthy mode of dressing the hair of women, especially young ones, is to let the hair be as loose as possible, or arranged in large bands, so as to allow the air to pass through them. It is a mistake to plait tightly the hair of children under eleven or twelve

105

years of age. The process of plaiting more or less strains the hairs in their roots by pulling them tight. The hair of girls should be cut at the ends, and allowed to curl freely."

❊ ❊ ❊

"The vessel that no woman objects to embark in — A *court-ship.*"

❊ ❊ ❊

Recipe For A Modern Bonnet

Two scraps of foundation, some fragments of lace,
A shower of French rosebuds to droop o'er the face;
Fine ribbons and feathers, with crape and illusion,
Then mix and *de*range them in graceful confusion;
Inveigle some fairy, out roaming for pleasure,
And beg the slight favor of taking her measure;
The length and the breadth of her dear little pate,
And hasten a miniature frame to create;
Then pour, as above, the bright mixture on it,
And lo! you possess "such love of a bonnet."

Anon.

❊ ❊ ❊

Zouave styles became popular during the sixties, with some blousing pants, shirts, and jackets. The one illustrated below is intended for a little girl, though a larger model could suit a woman just as well. It is in silk, embroidery, and braid.

❊ ❊ ❊

On the opposite page is a pattern for an "undersleeve with a very open dress sleeve," like those which became incredibly flared at the

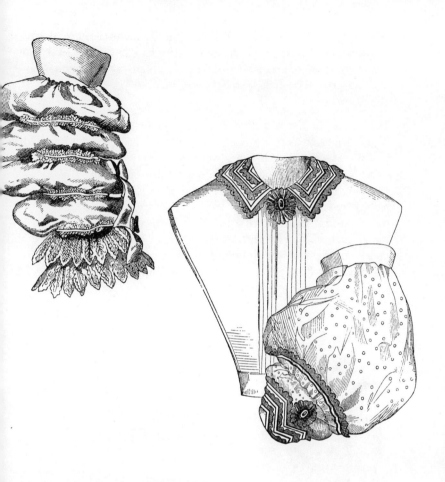

wrist. It is of a summer material. "Four puffs of Brussels net, separated by ribbon ruches, the two last terminating in bows on the forearm. Double fall of *point Duchesse*. This is a very suitable sleeve for the clear white muslin spencers so desirable for those to whom the Zouave jacket is unbecoming." The other is a collar and sleeve for half mourning and in June 1861 was considered very stylish.

✿ ✿ ✿

"Let no woman suppose that any man can be really indifferent to her appearance. The instinct may have been deadened in his mind by a slatternly, negligent mother, or by plain sisters, but she may be sure it is *there*, and, with a little adroitness, capable of revival. Of course, the immediate effect of a well-chosen feminine toilet operates differently in different minds. For some it causes a sense of actual pleasure, in others a consciousness of passive enjoyment; . . . None can deny its power over them, more or less; or, for their own sakes, had better not be believed if they do."

* * *

The article below is a new and easily made style of drawers from 1861. The article seems more utilitarian than decorative, and that it was. Most undergarments were made of cotton or linen as this one. Not until the eighties did they have frills, soft silk, or lace. Only in the forties were drawers generally coming into fashion, having been constructed as two open seamed legs attached by a waist band. They normally ended below the knees, the height rising gradually until the seventies, when they finally reached the knee. On the example shown, an inset of ribbon around the bottoms was the only decoration, the top being pulled tight by strings.

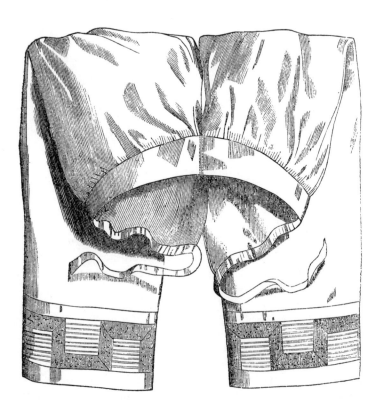

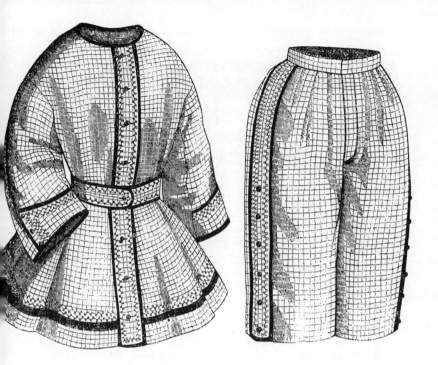

Above is the Garibaldi suit, styled and named, of course, after the great Italian patriot. It became a fad during the sixties, catching on somewhat more quickly, as was usual, on the continent and in England, before it reached the United States. The inspiration initially came from Garibaldi's famous red shirt, surfacing as a loose and informal blouse of red cashmere with front fastenings. Later the material was white cambric or muslin and was usually worn with a Zouave jacket. The suit, as well as various parts of it and the blouse, was equally popular for children's clothes.

* * *

On the following page is a *berthe* of thin muslin and "trimmed with puffs, with rows of black velvet between them. The lower part of the bertha is cut in waves, edged with a worked ruffle, and on each wave is a black velvet rosette."

* * *

The spencer is one of those fashions whose name has found its origin in a personage who knowingly or unwittingly has created a

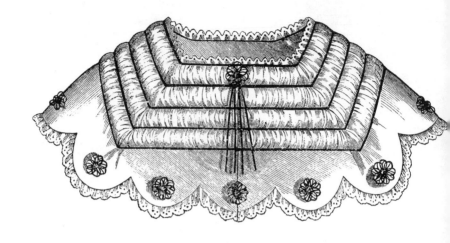

new style. Lord Spencer, George John Spencer (1758–1834), a fastidious gentleman, and a practical one, accidentally created the fashionable jacket so popular during the nineteenth century. One day, as the story goes, Lord Spencer, warming himself in the usual manner with his back toward the fireplace, found to his chagrin that his tails had caught fire. After the blaze was extinguished, he removed the charred coat and gave it to the valet, with instructions to trim it and hem the coat. The new style was an instant success, though Lord Spencer, wending his way to an important meeting, thought only of the practicality and necessity of the alteration.

✿　✿　✿

Opposite is a "neck-tie of green silk; the part going under the collar is cut to fit the neck; the ends are embroidered with gold braid, and trimmed with black lace." The lower one is of cherry colored silk. The ends are embroidered with gold braid and spotted with gold beads or bugles.

✿　✿　✿

Godey's constantly received praise from all inhabited corners of the country. One subscriber, writing in lieu of his wife, however had some sarcasm to level at the fashion plates, speaking as a man of Tennessee: "The great objection to the Monthlies of Chestnut Street is their plates. Each has generally thirty-six plates a year — women and children. Now, these may be scarce on Chestnut Street, but they are not so here. Now, can't you throw in a little variety — say a loafer, a bank director, a starved poet, an omnibus boy, or a cab driver, or any thing that is not common in the West?"

* * *

Many will think that the foolish and gullible young ladies of the era took to heart recipes which were either dangerous or unworkable, when in fact the potions, with some few exceptions were very useful. A friend of my acquaintance still, though she is much older than any of us, persists in using the oil of almonds and melted wax mixed for a beneficial handcream, cheaper by far than any of those touted on the market. Another, as I also have tested, can affirm the verity of the following: "To Remove The Odor Of Onions From The Breath. —

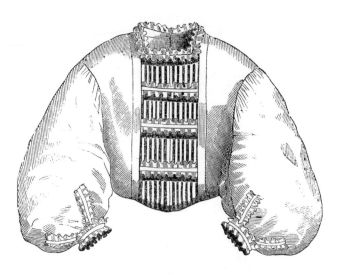

Eat a little fresh parsley or orris-root; it will effectually remove it."
Orris root can be purchased at any shop specializing in herbs.

❉ ❉ ❉

The shirt above is intended to be worn with a Zouave jacket. It
has a square neck and is trimmed with a fluted ruffle. The bosom
is formed of plaits and small fluted ruffles.

❉ ❉ ❉

Opposite are new drawers for misses of the same general style
illustrated previously, but trimmed a trifle more elaborately with
lace and ribbon or inserting. These particular examples are closely
approaching the knee in length.

❉ ❉ ❉

How shall we describe the caps of the sixties! They were certainly
popular and often followed the lines of a coronet frame with trimmings of lace, feather, or ribbon. Those on page 116 are of that
type. There were also the caps shown earlier, fauchons of lace and
cambric, often decorated slightly to give some color, with ribbon
and embroidery. They were either triangular or diamond shaped
pieces for a base, with the frippery attached. Some had lappets
which would be tied under the chin or under the chignon, which
grew in size during the era as the size of the caps diminished.
There are very few brims, possibly to make the wayward look a little
easier to catch.

"Redness In The Face. — A Tablespoon of gin thrown into luke-warm water will remove redness in the face produced by exertion."

"To Clean White Ostrich Feathers. — Four ounces of white soap, dissolved in four pints of water, rather hot, in a large basin; make the solution into a lather. Introduce the feathers, and rub well with the hands for five or six minutes. After this soaping, wash in clean water, as hot as the hands can bear. Shake until dry."

✿ ✿ ✿

Pictured below is a coronet "composed of black velvet, with three pearl or gold stars, a large one in the centre and a smaller one on either side. Two long white ostrich feathers, fastened in at the side of the coronet and crossing behind complete this coiffure. It would be equally pretty made in pink and blue velvet, with the feathers of the same color, the stars being made of pearl, studded with steel."

Below is a rear view of a different coronet, one of "black velvet . . . standing high in front and trimmed in black velvet leaves veined with gold, and mixed with gold tendrils or sprigs." It is also intended for fancy wear and can be made at home.

* * *

"Each lady should consider her own form, features, and complexion, and when she finds the prevailing modes do not suit her style, let her learn how to vary and improve, only bearing in mind, that *delicacy must never be violated, health never sacrificed, and propriety never disregarded.*"

* * *

"A young lady — a sensible girl — gives the following catalogue of different kinds of love: 'The sweetest, a mother's love; the longest, a brother's love; the strongest, a woman's love; the dearest, a man's love; and the sweetest, longest, strongest, dearest love — a love of a bonnet.'"

116

Four varying styles of hats and bonnets from the early sixties: at bottom opposite is a dress cap, with "mob crown of thulle. The front which terminates in long lappets, is of blonde; bow of black velvet ribbon, trailing half wreath of leaves, flowers, and berries." At far left is a cap for a young matron. It is of lace and net. Fashion indicated caps of this sort only for matrons and made them taboo to unmarried ladies. Above opposite is the popular "white chip bonnet trimmed with lilac ribbon and flowers." Above is a summer hat of brown leghorn, "trimmed with a very full brown feather and black velvet ribbon."

* * *

"Every young lady should be taught that all the muscles of the body may be made more strong by judicious exertion," wrote a physician to *Godey's,* continuing: "that those of the breast and shoulders require it more than any others, as they are the first to exhibit weakness, if neglected, and also they are the most important. Look at a girl whose exercise is limited to an occasional promenade or dance; you will find her shoulders round and her body stooping; or you will perceive that in the absence of all muscular ability to sit upright, fashionable dress has intervened to correct the deformity produced by idleness. The complaint is often heard that females are weak without the support of dress. The truth is, they have taken from the frame its uniform action, and have transferred to articles of apparel those duties which belong entirely to the muscles which God created for certain well known definite purposes."

❀ ❀ ❀

"The Elsie" is "an easy apron for a child, suitable for a little party. It is made of cerise silk, trimmed with graduated ruffles, and ornamented with rosettes of silk or ribbon." Opposite is a woolen knit knee warmer, considered to be very comfortable in chill weather.

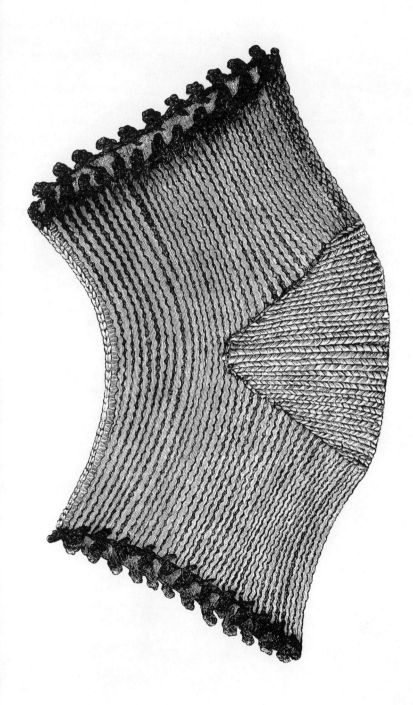

119

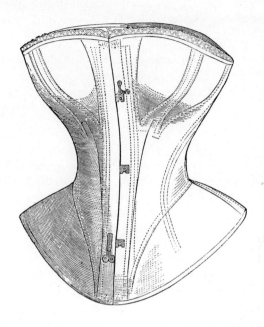

Opposite is a purse for a lady or gentleman from January, 1842. It is crocheted and has tassels. It is approximately three-quarter to full size and normally would have a ring of steel, though pearl and other materials could be used, to fasten it; the style is the familiar stocking purse or miser purse. Its form is not specifically nineteenth-century. Long purses were certainly used in the eighteenth-century toilets, but the usual means of carrying necessaries was a pocket. During the years in which large skirts were the fashion, pockets were the purses. Later, when skirts diminished and the number of necessaries increased, net purses of plain silk or heavier mesh with a single clasp became fashionable. Often they took the form of bags held by a waistband and were called chatelaine bags; later they were made of leather and silk over a frame of metal. Almost all of them were lined richly to contain the powder puff, a lady's opera glasses, snuff, and all of the normal items that found their way into purses.

❋ ❋ ❋

The corset above is, for the early sixties, a new style of the Victoria Corset. The busk is a steel clasp, for easy removal and fastening.

"Cleaning Hair Brushes. — It is said that soda dissolved in cold water is better than soap and water. The latter very soon softens the hairs, and the rubbing completes their destruction. Soda, having an affinity for grease, cleans the brush with very little friction."

* * *

The oversleeves below indicate the general mode of wear. Undersleeves previously illustrated were worn underneath, both for warmth and hygienic purposes. They were an added decorative effect, in addition, adding to the flare of the outer sleeve as well as diminishing the apparent size of the hand.

* * *

The hair ornament on the following page is intended for evening wear and is described as "very simple, and generally becoming. The

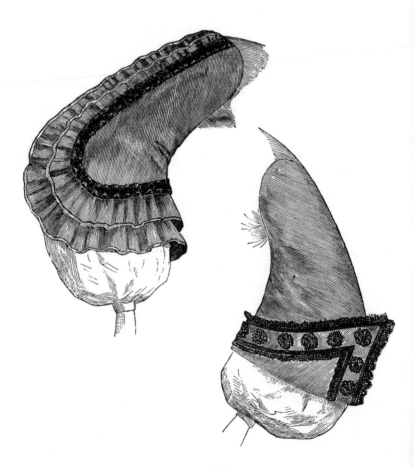

rosettes are formed of pieces of bias silk, about an inch and a half in width; the edges are cut out in points, and the silk box-plaited and formed into a rosette, then sewed on to stiff net; the band can be of velvet or silk, and a bow of ribbon to match the silk is often placed on one side of the band. One or more colors can be used; rose sublime and black make a good contrast."

* * *

"What is the shape of a kiss? — A lip tickle."

* * *

"Example For The Ladies. — Mrs. Mary R. Hubbard, Troy, N. Y. earned with a Wheeler & Wilson in 1868, $731.47; stitching 31,092 shirt-fronts, equal to 886,122 feet of seam. At 20 stitches to the

inch, this would give 212,669,280, an average of 708,891 per day, 88,612 per hour, and 1477 per minute, or sixty times as fast as hand sewing. Sixty years in one! The machine has run three years by steam and three by footpower without repair, and is as good as when bought."

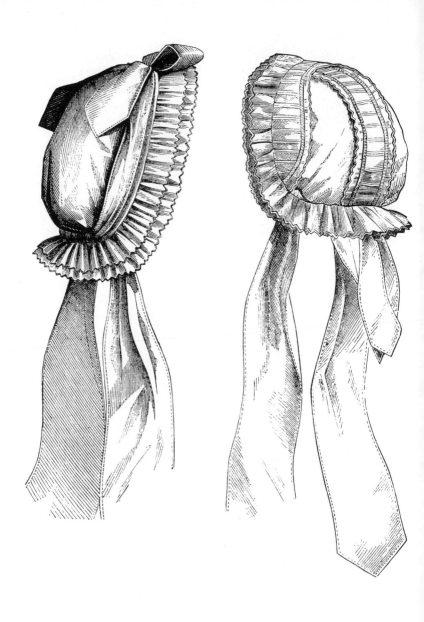

Above are the typical styles of night caps mentioned previously, these from March, 1862. The neck piece to the right is the "Victoria Tie." "The band of the neck is shaped out to fit. It is made of silk, and covered with lace; the ends are of lace, but the centre part is lined with a bright-colored silk, the same as the band."

125

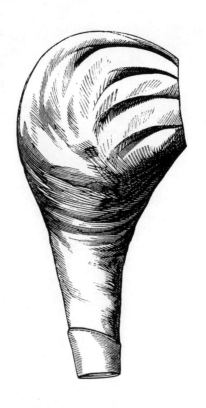

In 1862, fashion intelligence in *Godey's* informed readers of a fashion from the thirties making its reappearance. There seems to be little evidence that the style was any more than a fad and relatively short-lived: "The gigot, or 'leg of mutton,' sleeve, which used to be such a favorite with our grandmothers, has now come into fashion again, and is a style which is more used for morning wear than any other. It is very simple in its construction, being cut in one piece, with a *very decided* slope at the top, and, when pleated in to the armhole, very much resembling the shape of a leg of mutton. It is made to fit tightly to the wrist, being fastened by means of buttons and loops, or hooks and eyes, over which a pointed white linen cuff should be worn. We have illustrated a plain gigot sleeve as being the easiest to make, but they are also worn trimmed in a variety of ways, and are much more elaborate in their construction."

❧ ❧ ❧

To the right is a design for embroidery of initials in a vignette of a butterfly, a favorite motif of the era. The design here is intended for

126

the corner of a handkerchief or made larger to serve as the design
for a pen wiper.

* * *

"Stains Caused By Mildew. — Mildew is removed in several ways
from linen. Some dip the article in sour butter-milk, lay it in the sun
to whiten, and then wash in clean water. Others apply soap and
chalk, or soap and starch, and the juice of a lemon."

* * *

On the following pages is the favorite combination style of the
Zouave jacket and Garibaldi shirt. The shirt is pleated white
cambric, edged with lace, or of lace and red silk. The jacket is of
white piqué, with black silk embroidery and black braid trimming
the edges.

127

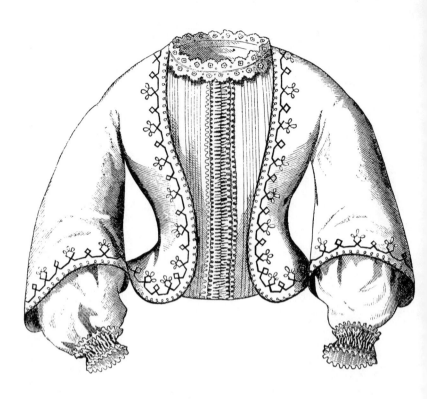

Opposite is a fancy "coat for a little boy, made of fine gray cloth, and braided with heavy black cord." The opera hood is of white merino and cherry silk braid.

* * *

Children's fashions of the fifty-year period are peculiarly interesting because of the reflections of adult fashion which they present. Often the adult fashion, as in the case of pantalets, was tested and exposed to public eye on the child first; after acceptance was partially accomplished, the adults donned the mode. For a general view of what a little girl's dress looked like, however, the common rule was imitation of the mother. Children of both sexes, with little differentiation, were dressed approximately alike until they were about six-years-old. Both boys and girls wore frocks with skirts which were often embroidered, ribboned, and frilly. The boys were an exception in that they rarely were made to wear the crinoline. Before and after that magic age, hats were worn by both, the material usually straw in summer and felt or wool in winter. After the skirts were taken off the young

128

gentlemen, they followed the general mode of their fathers, wearing trousers, jackets — though tailless — and hats. By the sixties, the popular knicker style was a common garment. With the girls, the skirts generally followed the lines of the mother's, being looped up during the seventies and slightly bustled, crinolined during the duration of that style, and only differed drastically earlier, the general style in the thirties or forties being a short skirt with long, ankle length drawers. Aprons were frequently worn for their protective qualities.

* * *

Fashion's extravagance, the "conspicuous consumption" of Thorsten Veblen, had reached phenomenal levels by the late sixties. Earlier, John Watson in his *Annals* had written: "The daughter of a merchant of my acquaintance, who was married at Philadelphia in 1835, had her wedding wardrobe furnished at a cost of 1000 dollars; her robe was fringed with gold, her pocket handkerchief, by reason of its

129

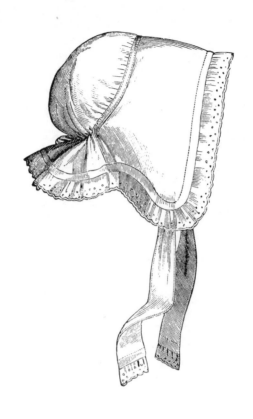

130

gold hem and decoration, cost 30 dollars! What an advance of style since the war of Independence!" But his fears would have grown had he seen the extravagance thirty years later. The cost had almost doubled and would continue growing.

* * *

Illustrated opposite are a plain night cap and a baby's boot embroidered in silk. The basic material of the bootee is white cashmere. It has a cambric lining, with blue silk decor.

* * *

"How To Dress For A Photograph. — A lady or gentleman, having made up her or his mind to be photographed, naturally considers, in the first place, how to be dressed so as to show off the best advantage . . . Orange color, for certain optical reasons, is photographically, black. Blue is white, other shades or tones of color are proportionally darker or lighter as they contain more or less of these colors . . . Complexion has to be considered . . . Violent contrasts of color should be especially guarded against. In photography, brunettes possess a great advantage over their fairer sisters. The lovely golden tresses lose all their transparent brillancy, and are represented black; whilst the 'bonnie blue e'e,' theme of rapture to the poet, is misery to the photographer; for it is put entirely out. The simplest and most effective way of removing the yellow color from the hair, is to powder it nearly white; it is thus brought to about the same photographic tint as in nature. The same rule, of course, applies to complexions. A freckle quite invisible at a short distance is on account of its yellow color, rendered most painfully distinct when photographed. The puff-box must be called in to assistance of art."

* * *

From time to time the editor of *Godey's* or the publisher would notice and print fashion intelligence from abroad. One such item had appeared in the London papers and read partially: "False ears of flesh color — India rubber — have been invented for the use of ladies with large ears. They are used in front of the real ears, which are drawn back and concealed under the hair." It was nothing new in the late sixties to see such correctives to nature on the market. Beyond the absurdity of the false ears, however, were also false lips, necks, and busts. The editor could only comment that with the

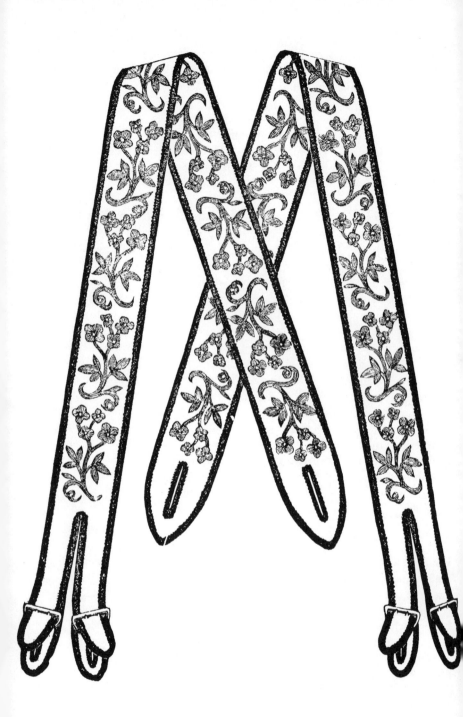

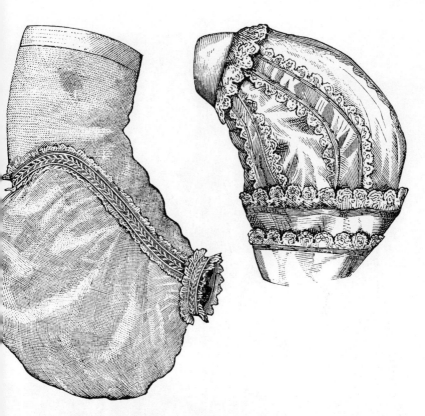

notice of false calves for sale in Philadelphia, and those false teeth and the artificial hair of the past, it was a "pretty good assortment of falsities."

❀   ❀   ❀

Godey's was much the seamstress' book as well as the home crafts-woman's. Many of the foregoing and following articles could be made at home, in some instances with full directions given to the lady of the house, in others only by way of suggesting the method. Pictured to the left is one such article, braces for a beau or husband. They are crocheted elastic and are made of cerise and white Berlin wool.

❀   ❀   ❀

Above are two styles of dress sleeve suggested for the spring of 1863. Both are suited to either light or heavy materials and are edged and trimmed with lace. The one on the right is intended for dress or evening wear.

134

The closer one approached the seventies, the closer one advanced toward an age of disguise — disguise of almost every article imaginable. There were the famed dresses on table legs, crocheted wastebasket covers, smelling bottles, and pen wipers. The item to the left is a pen wiper disguised ingeniously to appear a miniature parasol. The style is consistent with parasols of the day: a carved, highly ornate handle, ribboned and fringed edge, and beaded, embroidered, or bugled body.

*　*　*

In the last half of the century corset covers, like that illustrated below, became popular and replaced the earlier chemise. This undergarment would later evolve into the camisole, by the addition of a slightly longer waist. The cover was often made of flannel or fine cambric muslin as the one illustrated. They were trimmed with embroidery or lace.

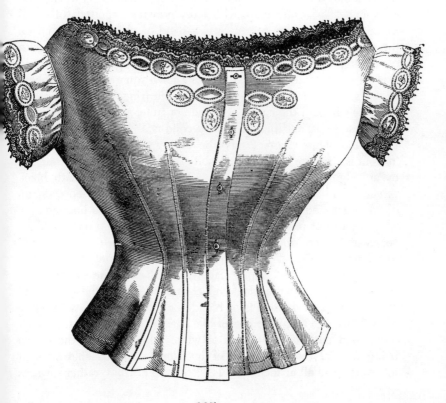

Bonnets and hats from the mid-sixties: from left to right, the first is a bonnet "of white chip, with loose crown of spotted tulle: all round the upper edge of crown is a band of plaid ribbon, and on the top part of the crown is a half diamond of tulle, edged with plaid ribbon, and a chenille fringe to match the plaid. The curtain is of white lace, and has in the centre a small square of plaid ribbon, edged at the bottom and sides by chenille fringe. The strings are of white silk, and the cap is of blonde or tulle, and is trimmed with roses, rose-buds, and bluets." The second is a "Mousquetaire hat of Leghorn or white straw. Round the hat is a scarf of blue ribbon, . . . in front is a rosette of black and white speckled feathers, surrounded by an edging of blue flowers . . . The brim is edged with black velvet." The third is a "black crinoline bonnet, with loose crown of white spotted tulle; the crown is divided from the bonnet by a shaped piece of pink silk, edged at the bottom with a narrow black velvet and a jet fringe, and having in the centre a group of white roses, rose-buds, and a few tufts of grass; the front of bonnet is finished by a narrow guipure lace turned back. The curtain is of pink silk, edged with a black velvet and jet fringe; the strings are of pink silk, and the cap is of blonde or tulle, trimmed with white roses, buds, and a few fullings of black lace." Next is a dress bonnet, "composed entirely of fullings of white tulle, those on the crown being formed into a species of *bouillons,* divided lengthwise at intervals by small artificial pearls; at the top of front, rather towards

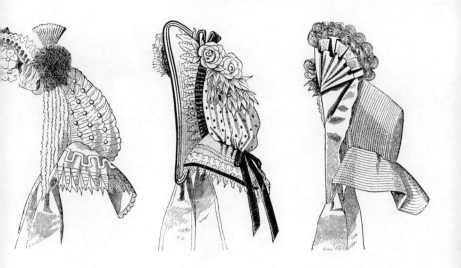

the left side, is a group of green leaves, with a tuft of white silk or feathers; the curtain is formed of broad white lace. The strings are of white silk, and the cap is of blonde, trimmed at top with a group of large white flowers." The fifth example is an elegant bonnet of "white chip, with loose crown of spotted net; the crown is separated from the front of bonnet by a black velvet, edged with black lace; . . . the front edge is bound with black velvet, close to which are two rows of narrow black velvet. The strings are white, and the curtain is covered with black lace, and has a bow and long ends of black velvet at the back. Cap of blonde, trimmed with roses and buds." The last is a "Leghorn bonnet; the front edge trimmed with a shaped piece of maize silk, plaited like a fan toward the top; at the top is a plume of maize ostrich feathers. Strings of maize silk, and blonde cap with a few roses and rose-buds."

* * *

"A New York milliner has built a bonnet which is a marvel of cheapness at $125," read the 1869 notice. The editor aptly damned the practice of escalating the prices of fashions, noting that those at home who were adept, could beat the couturiers at their own game.

* * *

"The dressing of the hair is of course a subject of importance, now that the back hair is no longer covered. The waterfall is the usual

style, and as some persons may be at a loss to arrange it, we will give them a hint on the subject. Tie the back hair rather low on the neck. If a braid is required, tie it under the natural hair, letting it rest on the neck. Then roll the front hair and fasten the ends at the back. Comb the front locks, which are fastened at the back with the back hair. Pin on a frizette and turn the hair up over the comb,

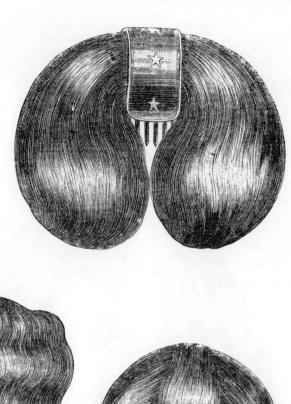

which must be entirely concealed. Then put on a net and tie a
ribbon round the waterfall."

* * *

On the page opposite are false plaits of hair, worn with the knot
just over the brow. Left above is a "waved waterfall, with ball comb

139

140

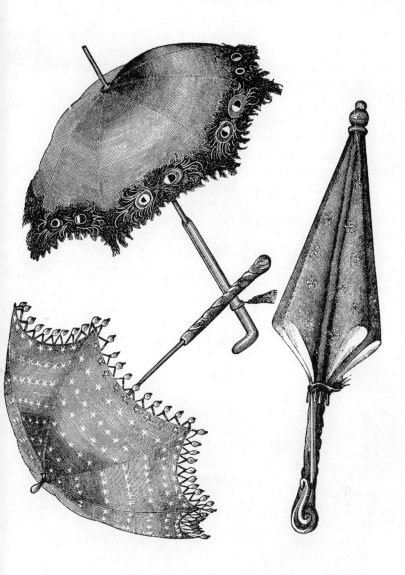

and fancy clasp of jet and gold." The second is a "new style of hair bow, very pretty for a ball coiffure." The third is a "waterfall bow caught with a fancy clasp comb."

❋ ❋ ❋

A Zouave robe of cuir-colored percale, stamped with a design representing braiding in black, is illustrated to the left. Above are three fancy parasols from the sixties: "One is of pink satin, ornamented with crystal and gold beads, sewn on in the form of stars, and added to the fringe; another is in white satin, bordered with peacock feathers; and the third is of violet silk, ornamented with mother of pearl bugles."

❋ ❋ ❋

"This style boot or short gaiter is very much in fashion, and looks particularly neat and pretty for children. It is made of white piqué, lined and quilted; each part of the boot is bound with fine white braid. It is fastened at the side with round pearl buttons, and a rosette of white gimp cord finished off with tassels is placed at the top in front." This style follows adult dress in two basic ways; it is tasseled at the top and has side buttons. The fashion is particular to the late sixties.

❋ ❋ ❋

The hat opposite is the "Chapeau Bavarois. This convenient country hat is of coarse white straw, trimmed with a broad black velvet studded with field daisies."

"Harrison's Parian White gives to the complexion the rich tone of the Parian marble . . . Carnation Rouge, for the cheeks and lips; a pure delicate, permanent rose tint . . . Superfluous Hair Removed from any part of the body in *five minutes, without injury to the Skin,* by 'Upham's Depilatory Powder' . . . Aromatic Vegetable Soap. A Superior Toilet Soap, prepared from refined Vegetable Oils, in combination with Glycerine, and especially designed for the use of Ladies and for the Nursery. Its perfume is exquisite, and its washing properties unrivalled."

❀ ❀ ❀

"Nothing is considered of more consequence in the feminine toilet than the fashion of a cap, especially as a part of a bridal wardrobe, or of the preparations for an invalid's room, especially if the convalescent be a young mother, receiving the congratulations of her friends and acquaintances."

❀ ❀ ❀

"A profusion of buttons, and cords, and gimps, is never in good taste, or, more especially, a mixture of the three. An undue quantity of braiding always gives a tawdry effect, reminding one of the 'infant phenomenon,' whose nankeens were 'bedecked with braids, buttons,

143

and gingerbread.' For little boys hovering between dresses and the first pair of 'pantaloons,' we recommend short trousers or drawers of white linen, and cambric sacques of plain colors, pale green, blue, pink, or buff, with a narrow edge of white braid in parallel rows. They should be made low in the neck, very loose, and with short sleeves. A broad belt of patent leather will confine them sufficiently at the waist. For the street, high brown-linen aprons, of sacque pattern, are a sufficient protection, the belt to be worn upon the outside, sleeves long."

Above and to the left are various ornaments of flowers made up at home and from any kind desired. Upper left is a breastpin, below it a bracelet. The comb above is decorated for evening wear.

❀ ❀ ❀

On the following page is a fancy belt, constructed of some pretty colored belting, ornamented with bead and bugle work. The deep fringe is of beads and bugles. Above it is an ornament for the neck, a "Cross, In Card And Beads." The materials are narrow velvet, perforated card, beads, and silk. The construction is simple: "Cut perforated card in the shape of the design shown in the engraving.

145

Two corresponding pieces of each shape will be needed, which should be ornamented according to the design, with beads, then placed on each side of the velvet and stitched upon it with silk. The velvet is also dotted over with beads."

* * *

"Comfort For The Calumniated. — The fairest complexions get freckled the soonest."

* * *

"It is a generally understood thing, and indeed almost a matter of necessity to ladies with large visiting lists, that calls, unless from the most intimate friends, are confined to reception days." A lady, let us assume Mrs. Smith, would at the beginning of the season leave her card with the notice that she would be "in" on Thursdays. "Mrs. Smith's general acquaintances, then, will understand that they will find her at home, and at leisure to see them on Thursday until three, or five, as her dinner hour may be. Usually the lady of the house is in an ordinary visiting dress." Later the custom became a fashionable one, with the hostess in full dinner dress and the visitors in a light carriage outfit.

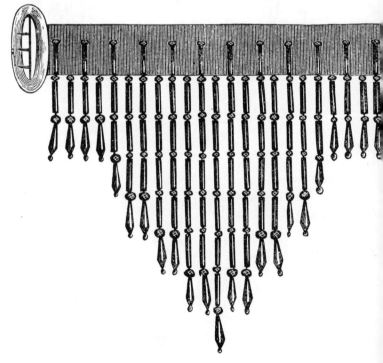

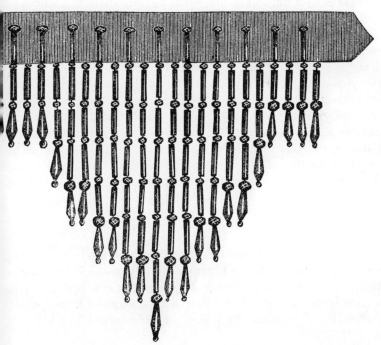

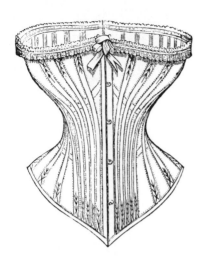

Doctors were extremely fond of criticizing corseting, their letters and advice appearing frequently throughout the entire history of *Godey's*. A typical admonition read: "The grand hygienic problem of a *corset without danger* will probably forever remain unsolved ... What is most singular is, that women are aware of the injuriousness of the corset — they instinctively feel that its action is an unnatural and eminently hurtful one. Here is the proof. If, by accident, a lady falls ill in a crowded assembly of any kind, a general cry is raised by the others, 'Cut her lace!' This is done instantly — the compressing machine is opened, air rushes into the lungs, the victim breathes, and recovers — which, however, will not prevent her recommencing the next day, so inexorable and powerful is this malicious demon — fashion." So concerned were they with the evils of the corset, that throughout the century many diseases were thought to be the result of the practice, among them pneumonia, curvature of the spine, pain in the head, ears, and throat, whooping cough, apoplexy, faulty vision, and consumption.

❀   ❀   ❀

The corset above is the most famous and perhaps the best advancement made in corsets during the era. The "Thomson's Patent Glove-Fitting Corset" was manufactured by America's largest firm and featured front snaps as well as a latch that prevented it from opening accidentally. It eliminated the busk, or wide bone which held the

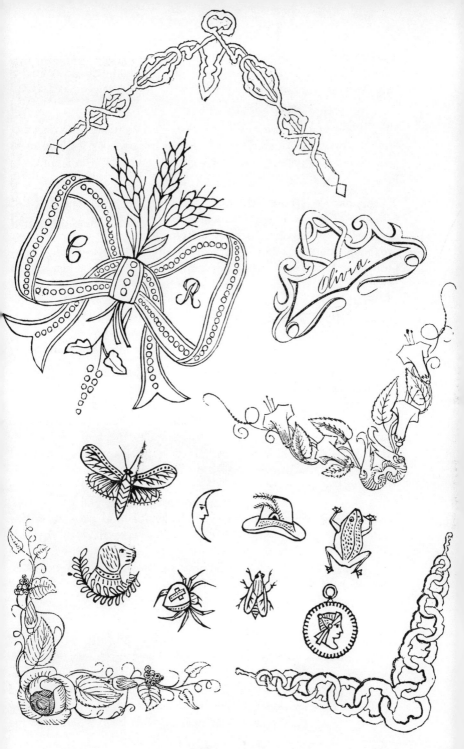

149

abdomen in and was consequently more comfortable. Beside it is the "Patent Bon Ton Bustle," a frame popularized by the A. K. Young Company.

❀ ❀ ❀

The designs on the previous page are typical motifs used in decorating cambric handkerchiefs, most dating from the sixties, and used on men's and women's accessories alike.

❀ ❀ ❀

"Chignons. — A party of people went out for a sail one day last summer, but (as not unfrequently happens) the wind rose, and presently all the ladies felt very ill. One young lady was just about to 'go off,' and the sailor — a great rough man, of course, not accustomed to ladies — just put his arm so as to catch her head when she fell back in a faint. She had on a chignon, fastened with a beautiful tortoise shell comb, and this giving away, the whole thing fell into the sea. The sailor tried to catch it with his boat hook, but it was of no use, for the weight of the comb, sunk it. The other ladies of the party, who also felt ready to 'go off,' were alarmed by

this, and fearing they might lose their chignons too if they fainted, reserved themselves for a future occasion; in the meantime securing their chignons by holding them on." The curl chignon below is typical of the late sixties and is described as having a gordian knot.

* * *

Opposite is another fashionable parasol from the same period, this one of green satin and trimmed with chenille fringe. The bow on the top is of satin ornamented with small buttons and edged with fringe. It has a pearl handle inlaid with gilt.

* * *

"When a lady is in danger of drowning, raise her by the dress, and not by the hair, which oftentimes remains in the grasp."

* * *

"To Prevent Hair From Falling Off. — Cocoa-nut oil melted with a little olive oil, and scented as preferred. Sage tea is good for a wash; or warm water."

HE SEVENTIES saw an even greater expansion of the country and of American life. The telephone, phonograph, and light bulb were all invented during the decade. Thomas Hardy and George Eliot were read, as were Whitman, Twain, and James. Philadelphia would stage a monstrous exposition to celebrate the Centennial, and there the Franklin Institute would serve the first ice cream soda, an instant sensation.

The cost of living still rose and apparently the consumption of alcohol among women. Huge families were on the decline as well as a woman's servility to the home. Frequently stories of the unspeakable horror of marriage appeared in the news by those who would warn others. Prudishness reached a high point as did decoration. A woman would not complain about any ailment occurring between her neck and her knees. She disguised the chair, the table, the smelling bottle, the house, herself, everything. Architecture was genuinely "Victorian."

In fashion extravagance continued. A well dressed woman wore two skirts, whether she was in morning dress or bedecked for dinner or the dance. The top one was looped-up or tied behind her waist. It was usually gored and highly decorated with flounces, buttons, frills, or bows. The underskirt, no longer a legitimate underskirt, was plain. Aprons were popular. The bodice was tight and high. Jackets were frequently worn over. The bustle enjoyed its vogue, only drifting out of style near the end of the age. Crinolines became a popular mode near the end of the decade. Bonnets and caps continued small. The normal coiffure was generally curled and

152

pulled close to the head, with ringlets hanging down. Cosmetics and jewelry grew in popularity. Shoe-manufacturing, having grown in the previous decade, increased the popularity of boots. High heels were popular at one point during the time; skirts lifted a little to expose the fashionable foot. The best shape on the best dressed woman was small busted, small waisted, and big hipped.

* * *

The two fans above are styles from the early seventies. On the left is one with black lace leaves separated by carved and pierced gilt sticks. The other is one of delicately carved ivory, the leaves and sticks being both of ivory. It is fashioned to appear to be lace and is only moderately intricate in its decorative illusion.

* * *

Parasols usually increased in size as the bonnet decreased in its ability to protect the wearer from the sun. Consequently those of the earlier part of the century were smaller than those of the seventies. Ribs were often heavy in the beginning, being made from whalebone. Later steel ribs were manufactured and used to decrease the weight of the article. Cane often proved a cheaper substitute. The shade itself was often of satin or silk, feathered or fringed or ribboned on the rim. Embroidery and lace served as edging. Bugles and beads decorated the cloth. Handles were of carved wood, coral, ivory, mother of pearl or inlaid — in all, the object was elegant.

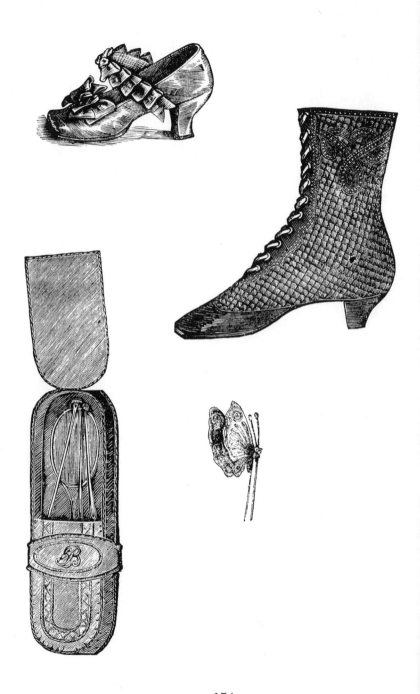

Corsets were not the only villains in fashionable circles. Tightly laced boots were often assailed as they became popular, especially in the late sixties and seventies. Like corseting, tightly laced boots or boots of absurd designs were blamed for apoplexy, consumption, hemorrhaging, and pains in the chest and stomach. The call went out for low-heeled and lightly laced boots. Nevertheless, manufacturers continued to produce according to fashion. A typical note appeared in 1869: "A San Francisco bootmaker has invented the latest agony in the way of ladies' gaiters. The heels, about two inches in length, taper down from the foot until they are no thicker than a man's thumb, and widen out again until a silver twenty-five cent piece, which is screwed on the bottom, just covers it."

* * *

Two styles of footwear from the seventies are pictured opposite: The first is from late in the era and is a "morning slipper of black kid; trimmed with ribbon bows to match the color of morning dress." The other is from early in the decade. It is of violet satin, lined with silk or satin and quilted. The two other illustrations indicate a hair ornament fashioned into a gold butterfly and a spectacle case covered in brown or black silk and neatly embroidered.

* * *

"Sewing On Black Cloth. — To remedy the difficulty which persons with defective eyes experience when sewing on black cloth at night, pin or baste a strip of white paper on the seam of black cloth to be operated upon; then sew through the paper and cloth, and when the seam is completed, the paper may be torn off."

* * *

Early in the seventies, another legitimate scare spread throughout the fashionable world. Women had been warned before about the effects of white lead used as a cosmetic. This time, the poisoning lay in the use of a fabric dyed a certain color. Two contributions to *Godey's* from 1870 and 1872 indicate the danger: "Green ball dresses are always much in fashion for the fair complexioned ladies whom they suit. But the bright green which looks so charming carries death with it, and the dressmakers, and the ladies who wear them, suffer from the effects of arsinate of copper which gives the much-admired dye" to the fabrics. The later testimonial offered much

more vivid proof, saying that "a lady in Mobile was not long ago made seriously ill by poison, manifesting itself by sores about the mouth, caused by biting her thread while working with green sewing silk."

❊ ❊ ❊

"Mrs. S. A. Moody's Patented Self-Adjusting Abdominal Corsets. *The only corset made upon correct principles.* The almost universal ill health of women has caused innumerable devices and appliances to be made and experimented with, and still the ills seemed not only to continue but increase. After a great deal of study and change . . . , this admirable and practical invention has been perfected, and its use has proved a blessing to many. Its adaptability, efficiency, and comfort demonstrate its value, and make it far superior to any corset or supporter ever before offered to the public. Thousands, unable to walk or take exercise of any kind, have been so remarkably relieved and benefited that their medical attendants have been constrained to adopt . . . this corset. It has been confidently stated, by the most eminent medical authority, that its universal use would make female diseases the exception, rather than the rule . . . It is simple and very substantial — gives uprightness and elegance to the form as well as elasticity and tone to the whole system, and is becoming universally popular with ladies."

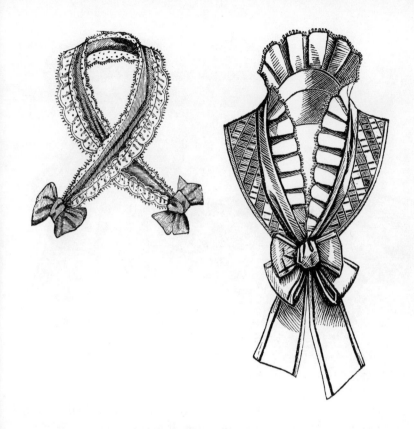

Above left is a "collarette to wear over a high neck or heart-shaped dress, made of pink china crape, laid in plaits, trimmed with Valenciennes lace; the sleeve is made of white lace to correspond." At right is a fichu of the late seventies, made of "plaid blue velvet and satin, trimmed with a plaiting of lace, and finished with a ribbon bow."

* * *

Ladies often wrote to *Godey's* for advice, to track down a style, or to get a recipe mentioned in daily gossip. One request elicited a large response, probably because the recipe was famous. Out of the large number of responses, the editor chose this item as the best recipe for "General Twigg's Hair-Color Restorative": "One drachm lac surphur, half a drachm sugar lead, four ounces rosewater. Mix

them, and shake the vial on using the mixture, and bathe the hair twice each day for a week, or longer if necessary."

❋ ❋ ❋

Fans reappeared in the forties to rival their eighteenth-century fore-runners, and increased in popularity until the end of the century. The two illustrated above were moderately decorative types for the mid-seventies. The one on the left is of white silk, "painted with colored flowers, and edged with white lace." On the right is one less frilly; its special feature being the silver cord from which it is suspended at the waist, a style common in the seventies. In basic construction fans were of two parts: sticks left plain or decorated, and leaves between. The sticks in the forties and fifties were distin-guished from those in fans later by being much narrower and in shape more delicate. They were of ivory, bone, wood, or mother of pearl, and were painted to contrast the scene on the leaves, to match it, or were gilded, worked in pierced designs, carved intricately, fretted, or plain. The leaves of the fan, however, were much more spectacular. Early in the era they appeared as vellum, painted with eighteenth-century pastoral scenes. For those who could not afford the vellum, paper was used. So popular did painted fans become, in fact, that many amateurs chose the craft as well as professionals. Later, silk, satin, feathers, and lace were used for the leaves. The silk and feathers were often delicately painted with scenes like those earlier in the century or with birds and flowers. Many of the fans were spangled, fringed, tasseled, or ribboned. Perhaps, the major exception to the general style of worked fan was the round or parasol fan, one which closed into its handle. Leather was often used for its construction. In all, the fan was among the most feminine and artful of fashions in the age, and despite its absence today still remains so.

* * *

Below are a brooch and earrings from the mid-seventies. They are silver with Bohemian garnets.

FIG. 20.

FIG. 21.

159

"Looped-Up Dresses. — A few days since we saw two ladies in Chestnut Street followed by a crowd. They took refuge in one of our large dry-goods houses, and had their dresses let down. The display was positively indecent. But fashion demands that dresses be looped-up, and the exposure is nothing." Looping dresses began as a style late in the sixties, extended into the seventies, and may be considered the precursor of the bustle. Skirts had been gored in front, allowing much fabric — a train — to begin extending to the back. The inconvenience of wet streets and dust was avoided by pulling the skirt back behind the waist and fastening them. The practice, as in almost every case when dresses are lifted, led to frillier petticoats and underclothes.

❋ ❋ ❋

The cap above left is a morning cap of white muslin, trimmed with a row of lace, a black velvet band, and loops of ribbon. To the right is an infant's hood of white satin, trimmed with white lace, blue ribbon, and feathers. At center is another morning cap. This one is

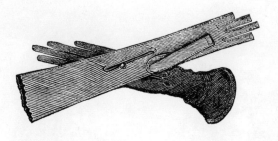

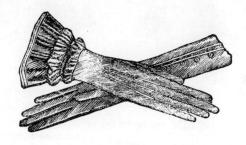

of white muslin, trimmed with lace and a pink silk ruché bows and
long ends.

❈　❈　❈

An editor of *Godey's* in the thirties noted that "a glove is an object
of luxury, elegance, and refinement," and so it was throughout the
century. They indicated, as a badge, the toilless life of the woman
who wore them, her class, and status. During many of the years,
in fact, a woman was seen indoors and out, gloved. Mittens were
worn indoors and for serving dinner, though one admonition, at
least, was made against the practice: "Particularly Addressed To
Ladies. — Dining in gloves is a vulgarity, and not allowable under
any circumstances." Those above are of spun silk, the upper ones
mittens and gloves for dress or informal wear; the ones below for
the evening. They are at the long length of the seventies, having
fluctuated during the century from very short to three-quarter to
full length.

The necktie at left is of "pink *crêpe*, trimmed with white lace; it is made up into a bow, the piece to go around the neck fastening it." On the right is a "rabat of Organdy muslin and lace. This rabat is made of two pieces of Organdy muslin, some Valenciennes insertion, and lace. The muslin is plaited perpendicularly, and the ends are sewn into a band, which is covered with a spray of convolvuli to match the bouquet."

✿ ✿ ✿

Opposite is a "black velvet bonnet, with silk crown, trimmed with black ribbon and feathers." To the right is one of white chip, "trimmed with white silk crown, and daisies around it; ribbon bow at the back." Below is a summer bonnet of chip for 1876.

✿ ✿ ✿

During the sixties and into the seventies, *Godey's* began to increase its services to its readers. An advertisement of that period announced that *Godey's* Fashion Editor would supply the following articles, at the prices listed, to anyone desiring them: *Infant's Wardrobe*: Dresses $4–40, Slips, $3–6, Double Wrappers $1–5, Cambric Nightgowns $2, Shawls, or Blankets $4–30; *Paper Patterns*: single $.60 — complete $5; *Knit Goods*: Split Zephyr Sacque for Infants, $2; Ladies' Breakfast Coseys $6, Ladies' Sontags $3.50, Ladies' Crochet Shawls $9–30; *Ladies' Ornamental Hair*: Grecian Curls, arranged on

162

comb $7–25, Hair Waterfalls $6–10, Puffs for Rolling the Hair $2–5; and many others. They also supplied complete wardrobes, trimmings, cloaks, jewelry, silverware, wedding and visiting cards, card cases, paper and envelopes, etc. etc. etc.

"Long words, like long dresses, frequently hide something wrong about the understanding."

* * *

To the left is a "cream-colored felt bonnet, trimmed with ribbon of the same shade, striped with brown velvet, long spray of different colored flowers and leaves; the same in the face." Below it is a bonnet of yellow straw, "trimmed with yellow ribbon edged with black; long ostrich feather, variegated flowers in the face."

* * *

Two fichus: the first is for evening and is made "of white French muslin, trimmed with lace; and silk band embroidered; it is fastened in front with a rose." The second is "trimmed with a puff, and lace fraise around the neck."

165

"Hoops for the communion table, made so as to make the dress set gracefully on the kneeling figure, is the latest development in fashion" in 1870.

✿   ✿   ✿

Pictured below are two fashionable parasols of silk with inset ivory handles. The two fans are of Russia leather, a material popular during the seventies. Both close into the handles.

✿   ✿   ✿

Stockings were as variable a fashion as any other. For the first part of the century, plain white or black, depending on the occasion, were the normal modes. They were usually made of silk or cotton. Late in the sixties and into the seventies, striped or colored stockings were much worn, like those intended for the boots on the following page. Many of them were open worked; some, especially toward the

eighties, were embroidered. Silk remained the most popular fabric. For dress, however, white stockings remained the proper color. Depending on the level of prudery throughout the century, pink or buff ones were worn under the white so as not to unduly expose the leg.

❊ ❊ ❊

Three styles of boots from the mid-seventies: the upper left is an infant's boot, somewhat reflecting the adult style. It is knit. To the right is a lady's boot of black kid, open up the front and fastened with buttoned bands to show the brightly colored stockings. The last is of French kid with a box toe. It is laced across the front loosely enough to expose the colored stockings.

167

"LADIES' TRAINS: —

GENERAL SUPERINTENDENT'S OFFICE

May, 1869

Rule 1: No train, after this date, will be made up of greater length than the height of the propelling power.

Rule 2: In coming down heavy grades (Church steps, for instance) first class trains will move as rapidly as safety will allow, but all accommodating trains will proceed slowly and stop frequently to allow people to step on the trains. Caution, however, is necessary in starting up whilst people are so engaged to prevent accidents.

Rule 3: All trains to be held up at crossings. All empty 'flats,' standing on the 'sidings' at the time, should be switched off.

Rule 4: When three or more trains are proceeding in company, they should always move side by side, and on no account whatever change this position. Trains approaching from the opposite direction must keep out of the way. (This rule is imperative.)

Rule 5: If it is desirable to attach a 'flat' to a moving train, speed should be slackened, and signals given by bowing. The 'flat' will respond by throwing away its cigar, twirling its moustache, and elevating its hat. The answering signal is a smile, which signifies 'couple on'; after 'coupling' the combined train will move off very slowly — very.

By order of   FASHION, *President*
A LA MODE, *Gen. Supt.*"

*   *   *

Opposite are a necklace of silver, one of black velvet with ornaments and a pendant of pearl beads, and finally, a costume for "girls of five years." It is a dress of gray linen, with a kilt skirt and a sacque, trimmed with scarlet and gray and bound in scarlet.

*   *   *

"A Pittsfield feminine Sunday-school teacher recently, while engaged in the administration of her duties lost her Bible and didn't know where to find it. When she got home the book of books was found wagging along on the bustle behind her, where it had been placed by a member of her class." The editor of *Godey's* promptly added: "By stiffening the article a little, teachers can carry small and invalid children on them." He also indicated that it would be good as an umbrella, to cover the toddler.

Below left is a fichu "made of white French muslin, plaited and divided by a band of cardinal silk and finished with a bow of cardinal ribbon." Next to it is a collar and revers of linen, "edged with narrow lace and ribbon bows. This is worn over an underwaist of white muslin, high neck and long sleeves."

❀ ❀ ❀

A fashionable lady almost always carried a fan, bouquet, or handkerchief, especially for formal dress. When fans were not the fashion the important accessory was the dear and elegant handkerchief. As fans increased in size during the century, as a general rule, the handkerchief decreased in its. During the thirties and forties it was extremely large. In the seventies it was approximately the size of a modern gentleman's handkerchief. The fabric was usually linen, cambric, muslin, or lawn. Depending on the occasion of dress, the handkerchief's style varied. For morning or day dress it could have

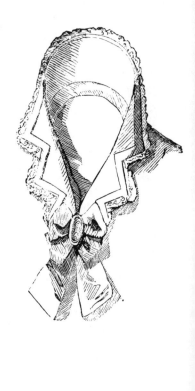

colored embroidery, though the coloring was a late development in decor and often considered in bad taste. For evening wear the handkerchief was always white, with white decor. Corners were rounded; edges were often scalloped; lace and crocheting often extended the hems. Sometimes all of the corners were embroidered with silk or satin stitching; more often only one was decorated. The motif was much like those scattered throughout the previous pages, sometimes a bug, a butterfly, sometimes an ornate initial supplied from an alphabet published in *Godey's* or another magazine, sometimes a floral pattern. They survive today, though much smaller, in the decorative handkerchiefs worn or carried by older women.

❈ ❈ ❈

The sleeve above is intended for a "costume in two materials. A deep cuff terminates the sleeve, and through this cuff a scarf of the contrasting material is passed, and tied on the outside of the arm; the arms are fringed out."

❈ ❈ ❈

Though the crinoline had generally disappeared during the seventies, there was still some use of the spring skirt or metal ribbed crinoline. Just as bustles were enjoying a diminished popularity toward the end of the decade, the crinoline began a slight popularity. One of the more famous was the J. W. Bradley, "Duplex Elliptic:" It "is not equalled in its wonderful flexibility and strength, its remarkable lightness, and natural elasticity experienced in all crowded Assemblies, Railroad Cars, Carriages, Church Pews, Armchairs, Pomenade,

171

or House Dress. It will not bend or break, like the single spring, and consequently preserves its perfect and beautiful shape more than twice as long as any other skirt ever made. It is the best quality in every part, and unquestionably the most graceful and elegant as well as the most comfortable, economical, and durable Hoop Skirt ever offered to the public. For children, misses, and young ladies, they are superior to all others. The hoops are all covered with two-ply double twisted thread, and will wear twice as long as the single yarn covering which is used on all single steel Hoop Skirts. The three bottom rods on every skirt are also double steel, and twice or double covered, to prevent the covering from wearing off the rods when dragging down stairs, stone steps, etc, etc., which are constantly subject to when in use. These skirts also measure in circumference at the bottom from two and a half to four yards."

*　*　*

The jewelry above is for mourning and is silver and jet. The vintage is approximately late seventies.

*　*　*

At the times when corseting was greatly in vogue and when minis-cule waists were much admired, a girl would be expected to have

172

a waist of 22 inches by the time she was sixteen and 16 inches by the time she was eighteen to twenty. Women often slept in their corsets to maintain the regimen. The most extreme example mentioned in *Godey's* was a waist of 12 inches. Thirteen-inch waists were not uncommon.

* * *

The shirts below were fashionable during 1877. The collars and undersleeves are made of linen and edged with lace and embroidery.

* * *

What did a woman read in *Godey's*? "Godey's Arm-Chair," "The Lily and The Sunbeam," "The Little Mourner," "Fashion Chit-Chat," crafts articles, "Center-Table," "The Bosom Serpent," "Fairy Land," "The Lone Woman," "The Way To Bring Him Back," "Julia In Consumption," "Autumn Musings," "How Would'st Thou Wish To Die?," "Some Remarks Upon German Drama," "Wait Ye Here While I Go and Pray," and many, many others.

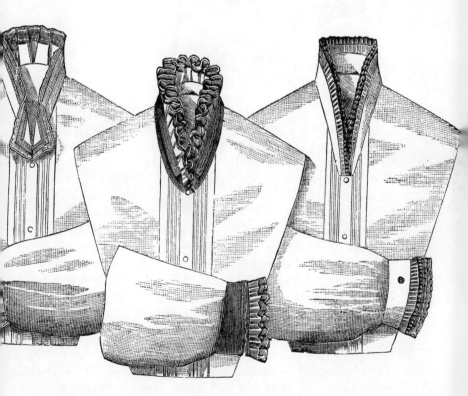

"There is no lock in the world which requires such a careful picking as wedlock."

❅ ❅ ❅

"Almond paste is of use in preserving the delicacy of the hands. It is made thus: Blanch and beat up four ounces of bitter almonds; add to them three ounces of lemon juice, three ounces of almond oil, and a little weak spirits of wine. The following is a serviceable pomade for rubbing the hands on retiring to rest: Take two ounces of sweet almonds, beat with three drachms of white wax, and three drachms of spermaceti; put up carefully in rose-water."

❅ ❅ ❅

The smelling bottle above is made as a smart chatelaine appendage in the shape of a dagger. It is of crystal glass and filagree silver.

Above left is a "bow for the throat of pink *crêpe de chine,* with lace ends, ornamented with pink braid and small tassels." Next to it is a "fan suspender made of colored silk braid, with ribbon bow at top, and the end where the fan is fastened on a hook." On the following page is a neck ornament of velvet ribbon an inch wide and "forty-four inches long, the center, and also the ends of which, are studded with steel spangles." On the last page is a child's hat of white straw, "trimmed with *écru* silk and cardinal wing." The other is of gray straw and blue wing and silk.

175

One of the more revealing stories of the foibles of nineteenth-century women's fashions concerns the lady to whom fashion was everything. She was past her prime, was not handsome, and wore things which made her less so. "It is the fashion," was her favorite saying. "One cannot go wrong when one is in fashion." Her friends would often taunt her: 'Even if the fashion is a ridiculous one?" She'd reply, "Fashion can never be ridiculous." "If it is unbecoming?" they would parry. "It is of no consequence," she would defend. "If it were directed to expose your throat?" "I would wear it so." "If you were to wear your dress to your knees?" "I would show them. I would always be in fashion." So it went, week to week, fashion to fashion. Her husband was patient, indulging her in her whims even though he realized her foolishness. One day he decided that it was time to teach her a lesson. He wrote and had published an article under a pen name for the special fashion magazine to which his lady subscribed. In it he described the latest rage in hair dressing. Some ladies, the article read, are now dressing their hair *a là Chinoise*, with fresh garden vegetables adorning the side of the coiffure for a unique effect, the more appealing of these being a carrot. Predictably his wife read the article and decided to wear her hair in the fashion to the Opera that evening. Her husband could hardly restrain his laughter, but he let her go her way. When she appeared that evening in her new, fashionable coiffure, the stares came, fans fluttered, and the conversation whispered. To her consternation, she met frowns. Silently comprehending the cause and resolving to be more discriminating in the future she asked her husband what was the matter. He replied, quietly assured she had learned her lesson: "My dear, a carrot does not become a blonde."

❁ ❁ ❁

The Lady's Book

The Lady's Book! How vastly rare
    Are the rich treasures gathered there!
It seems as if a fairy stood,
    With magic grace and lifted wand,
To give us everything of good
    That could be wafted by her hand.
And when we jest of fairy ken,
    And fairy freaks and fairy folk,
We ask no *better fairy* then,
    Than Godey of the Lady's Book.
We wish him many a happy year,
    From many a cozy quiet nook,
For charmed are thousands far and near
    In reading Godey's Lady Book.

Julia Louise Wheeler

INDEX

Poisonous dye 155.
Powdering 9.
Puffing (*See* Borrillonnées).
Purses 25, 43, 121; *illus.* 24, 42, 120.

Quilling 36, 37, 63.

Rabat 162; *illus.* 162 (*See also* Neckties).
Recipes 3, 18, 32, 35, 39, 58, 59, 65, 71–72, 106, 111–112, 114, 122, 127, 151, 157, 174.
Redingotes vi.
Redness in the face 113.
Ribbon vi, vii, viii, 24, 30, 31, 33, 36, 37, 38, 39, 41, 45, 53, 57, 58, 59, 63, 68, 69, 70, 72, 108, 112, 117, 123, 135, 136, 153, 155, 157, 160, 162, 165, 170, 175.
Riddles 10, 16, 32, 106, 123.
Riding habits vi.
Rings vii.
Ruffles vii, 16, 26, 32, 35, 68, 70, 109, 112, 118.

Sacque 144, 169 (*See also* Basque).
"Saragossa" 63–65; *illus.* 64.
Sartain, John 2.
Scallops 27, 29, 31.
Scarf 15, 38.
Scarlett O'Hara 66.
Screens (*See* Fans).
Serpent bracelets vi.
"Set" 39–41; *illus.* 40.
Sewing machine vi, 4, 9, 21; *"Old Fashion"* 70–71; *output* 123; *Singer* 70; *Wheeler & Wilson* 70, 123.
Shawls v, vi, vii, 10, 15, 16 (*See also* Capes, Cloaks, Mantles).
Shirts 127, 173; *illus.* 127, 173.
Shoe manufacturing 153.
Shoes v, 35, 35–36, 57, 155; *illus.* 36, 57, 154.
Silver 158, 159, 169, 172, 174.
Skirts v, vi, vii, 5, 9, 10, 16, 26, 29, 31, 34, 39, 52, 153.
Sleeves v, vii, viii, 9, 21, 26, 27, 29, 34, 39, 53, 57, 107, 122, 133, 171; *bell* 10; *leg-of-mutton* v, 9, 14, 126; *pagoda* vii; *illus.* 57, 107, 122, 126, 133, 171.
Smelling bottle 174; *illus.* 174.

Spectacle case 155; *illus.* 154.
Spencer vi, 107, 109–110 (*See also* Jacket).
Spencer, George John *Lord* 110.
Split straw 53.
Squirrel 15.
Suspenders (*See* Braces).
Stockings 166–167.

Tasseled boots viii, 142; *illus.* 142.
Taste 7, 14, 17, 36, 44, 59, 117, 143–144, 160, 171, 176–177; *among Philadelphia women* 33.
Tippets 15; *illus.* 15.
Tongue-twister 43.
Torsade vii.
Tortoise-shell combs v.
Trains viii, 169.
Trousers 62, 144.
Trousseau 23.
Tunic viii, 62; *illus.* 13.
Turquoise 28.

Undergarments 10, 53–54, 54–56, 108, 160; *illus.* 53, 108 (*See also* Corset, Chemisette, Drawers, etc.).
Underskirts vii, 27, 61, 152.
Undersleeves 10, 21, 27, 35, 53, 70, 106–107, 122; *illus.* 35, 70, 107.

Veblen, Thorsten 129.
Vellum 158, 159.
Verse 1, 2, 3, 5, 20, 106, 177.
Vests 28; *illus.* 28.
Victorianism 5.
"Victoria Tie" 124; *illus.* 125.

Waist size viii, 5, 172–173.
Watches vi.
Waterfall hair style vii, 66, 137–139, 139–141; *illus.* 139.
Watson, John F.: *Annals* 6; *remarks by* 12, 14–15, 44–45, 45–46, 129–131.
"White collars" 9.
White lead 33.
Women: *education of* 3–4; *professions* 4; *and sports* 3, 66; *shape of* vii, 21, 153; *special fares for* 37.

Zouave fashions viii, 66, 106, 107, 109, 112, 127, 141; *illus.* 106, 112, 128, 140.

MR. GODEY'S LADIES
Edited by Robert Kunciov

BONANZA BOOKS
NEW YORK

10

2 2 2 4 0